OUR JOURNEY
BY
B. J. BOHNE

IMPERIAL *Crane*

OUR JOURNEY
BY
B. J. BOHNE

Dr. Dennis Sempebwa

Eagle's Wings Press
"A Division of Hunter Heart Publishing" ™
Chicago, Illinois

To order products, or for any other correspondence:

Eagle's Wings Press: A Division of Hunter Heart Publishing™
1510 Chiles Ave., Suite 7
Fort Carson, Colorado 80913
www.hunterheartpublishing.com
Tel. (253) 906-2160 – Fax: (719) 358-9051
E-mail: publisher@hunterheartpublishing.com
Or reach us on the internet: www.hunterheartpublishing.com

This book and all other Hunter Heart Publishing™ books are available at Christian bookstores and distributors worldwide.

Edited by: Gord Dormer
Cover design & Photo layout by: Phil Coles Independent Design

ISBN: 978-1-937741-85-3
Printed in the United States of America.

IMPERIAL (im ˈ pi(ə)rēəl):

Majestic • Magnificent • Domineering

Dedication

*This book is dedicated to my father, John Bohne, who challenged me to become the man I am today.
I also dedicate this to the incredible team of men and women who have helped build Imperial Crane Services, Inc.*

– B.J. Bohne

Acknowledgements

I am profoundly indebted to our sales teams, administrators, crane operators, office staff, and all the incredible employees of *Imperial Crane*. You are the finest in the business!

I am grateful to our bankers, insurance companies, agents and dedicated clients. Without you, there would be no *Imperial Crane Services*.

Thank you to my dear mother Gayle for sacrificing personal ambitions and happiness for us. Your selfless commitment kept the family together and protected *Imperial Crane* from a myriad of destructive forces.

Thanks also to my big brother Lance Bohne for walking ahead of me and showing me the ropes. I will always admire your brilliance and quick wit. I pray the best for you always.

Special thanks to my younger brother Jonathan Bohne for your incredible ingenuity. I am confident that when it's all said and done, your impact on this company will propel our efforts to the next level.

To my lovely daughters Kailey and Willadene: thank you for changing my life. You have given me a purpose beyond myself. Daddy loves you immeasurably.

To my love Irena, thank you for the encouragement, support and friendship. You have helped me remain focused on what's really important.

I pay special tribute to my mentor, the late Jim Schmitz, for training and coaching me in the crane business.

Finally, to all the hands that have touched this project, thank you for your service and creativity. Without you, this book would never have come together.

Most of all, I am thankful to God who has favored me with wisdom, health, great relationships and the opportunity to impact others with the gifts He has graciously given to me.

Endorsements

Imperial Crane's level of excellence with regard to risk management is truly an amazing accomplishment. We have underwritten thousands of crane accounts since 1996 and rarely have we seen this type of favorable loss experience. This achievement is all the more significant considering the scope of Imperial Crane's undertakings, many of which include refineries and arduous City of Chicago projects.

~ National Builders Insurance Co.

We work exclusively with Imperial Crane on our jobs, and trust them to find the correct crane and layout for each task. We know the operators; we know their crew. When it comes to Imperial Crane, we are confident there will be no worries or issues. If we need a job done correctly, we call Imperial Crane. It's like pressing the "Easy" button.

~ Wigdahl Electric Co.

Whether it's a sixty-five foot man lift or a two hundred and twenty foot crane, Imperial Crane will take care of it, no matter what size the job. Their safety standards are simply the best!

~ Trinity Roofing & Sheet Metal

We come to Imperial Crane for several reasons, number one being they are a very competitive company. They have good operating engineers, very good equipment and a great safety record! I would certainly recommend Imperial Crane for any lift, any day!

~ AMS Mechanical

We generally don't do a lot of shopping around; we just pick up the phone and call Imperial Crane. They are simply reliable!

~ Intrinsic Landscaping

There is no job too large for Imperial Crane. They have a good, well maintained fleet. It's no wonder many large companies turn to them time and time again.

~ Morrison Construction

We are very proud to have Imperial Crane Services as a vendor. Their personnel, from the oiler on the crane to the man in the field, are very knowledgeable and professional; they are always willing to suggest the proper way to rig the lift and work in conjunction with our crew, no matter what the task. Thank you, Imperial Crane.

~ Orange Crush, LLC

Table of Contents

Prologue

It was a frosty Chicago morning when Dennis and I met at our favorite restaurant, Francesca's, in Palos Park, Illinois. After ordering the usual grilled tilapia with wild mushrooms and a leek cream sauce, he proceeded to share some highlights from his latest mission trip.

"Thanks for all your support, B.J.," he concluded. "But enough about me; what's going on with you? Business good?"

Well, a lot had been going on. Yes, business was good; very good in fact. I shared details with him of Imperial Crane's latest victories; we had recently negotiated a major contract and finalized consolidation of our financing. Our safety record was stellar, and we were making money. Yes, business was booming.

His eyes lit up. "B.J., you have to write a book!"

"Me? Write a book?" I mused.

Sure, I had a story: the Imperial Crane story. My mind began to reflect on the details of the journey, racing back through the incredible twists and turns. Yes, we've built a strong company. I took the reins of a good business, and by God's grace, my team and I have created something truly great.

Not all of the reminiscing produced positive thoughts, however. I remembered my father's call from Germany as if

Our Journey: By B.J. Bohne

it were yesterday. Weak and frail, his voice sounded nothing like the dynamic man I so admired.

"Dad, I'm coming to see you," I said firmly, anticipating a pushback. Normally he would have tried to dissuade me, especially since he was due back home in a week. But not this time; he simply didn't have the strength.

Twenty-four hours later my cousin Jeff and I were on a flight bound for Munich.

"I'm so glad you're here B.J.," he said, as he clung to me in a frail but warm embrace. Noticeably weaker, the aggressive treatments had clearly taken their toll. What had become of my strong, able-bodied father? I recalled our last encounter, days before he left for Germany, when he not only hugged me, but he also cried. That was a shock. I had never in my life seen my father cry. "Dad, you're only going to Germany for a month," I offered, trying to comfort him. "They'll give you the best treatment and you'll be back here in no time at all. Okay?"

Perhaps he knew the end was near.

The remote medical facility, nestled in a scenic town south of Munich, looked more like a bed and breakfast than the famed, cutting-edge cancer treatment center we understood it to be. Something must have been working, though, as his doctors were excited at his progress. They informed us he needed one more week to complete his first phase of treatments.

I convinced Dad that a few days away from the clinic would do him good. He could get away from it all and hang out with us. We checked into the penthouse suite at the

Imperial Crane

opulent *Kempinski Hotel Vier Jahreszeiten*, or *Four Seasons Hotel*, in the center of downtown Munich.

It happened that we arrived in Germany during Oktoberfest, the world's largest fair and largest beer festival. Known for its festive celebration of German culture, including oompah music and traditional food and costumes, it attracts more than six million people every year. Munich was definitely the place to be.

For the next few days, we did our best to forget about the medical facility we'd left behind. We sampled delicious German beers, savored traditional German cuisine and enjoyed the festival's inherent merriment.

Refreshed and revitalized, we were preparing to go out for dinner on our last night in Munich when the telephone rang. It was the Imperial Crane office back in Chicago. "Sir, the alarm was tripped this morning. It's okay; nothing is missing. It was Lance trying to get into the building. He has relapsed – again. He is really not doing well at all."

Dad loved Lance, much more than he publicly expressed, but when he received this news I could see the life drain out of him. For some reason, this was the proverbial straw that broke the camel's back. He was visibly angry and frustrated. His sense of utter helplessness is what seemed to hit him the hardest. For the first time, Dad could not fix this or anything else. Unbeknownst to him, he was teetering at the brink of death.

Right then, and seemingly out of nowhere, my uncle Jimmy Bohne, who had flown in to join us, turned to me and asked, "B.J., are you ready to take over Imperial Crane?"

Our Journey: By B.J. Bohne

Rather taken aback, I somberly replied, "I hope I don't have to. But if I do, I'm ready."

I don't think I convinced anyone. In fact, I don't think I quite believed what I was saying. The truth was, I didn't think I'd ever have to take over the company. As far as I was concerned my old man was coming back to work. In fact, the notion that Dad was not going to pull through was completely unthinkable.

Back in Chicago a week later, on October 9, 2003, having left Dad at the treatment center in Germany, I was enjoying a game of golf with some longtime friends at Butler National Golf Course. We were on the eighth hole when I got a call from the office. "Ugh . . . it's probably Dad again," I thought. Lately, he'd been on my case for not being in the office enough and for playing too much golf.

The call was from Bill Tierney, Imperial Crane's vice president. "B.J.," he said softly, "It's your dad. He just passed away."

The news hit me like a ton of bricks. I was dumbfounded; speechless. For a moment I forgot where I was. Time seemed to stand still, as an explosion of disparate thoughts raced through my mind. "No, this couldn't be," I agonized, "They must be mistaken. My father is dead? Not possible!"

As soon as I hung up I phoned my mother, Gayle. She began crying hysterically and immediately hung up on me.

I then phoned my younger brother, Jonathan. "No, wait," he pleaded, "You were just with him. What happened? You told me he was going to be okay!" Yes, I had told him Dad would be okay. I honestly didn't think he would die; not now.

4

Imperial Crane

Since my father's passing, I have taken the reins of the company. God has blessed Imperial Crane with phenomenal growth. We have ballooned into a $100 million, multinational corporation at the time of this writing. We have not only survived, but have thrived through the most trying economic times this country has seen since the Great Depression.

These thoughts were still circulating through my mind as my reminiscing began to come to an end. I pondered, "Who would want to read a book about some crane company? And even if I did want to share this story, I'm not really a writer."

"I'll help you put it together," Dennis said excitedly, as if he had read my mind. "B.J., you have a lot to share with the world. Your sacrifices, diligence, vision, and resolve have resulted in a remarkable business success story. You and I both know there's more to all of this than mere success. I really believe there's a world out there that will be inspired by your journey."

Without over-thinking the process, I enthusiastically agreed. And what a journey this has been.

Imperial Crane is a story of vision, conquest, courage and tremendous teamwork. It's also a story of pain, failures and setbacks. It's a story about life, really, which, as we all know, isn't always pretty. Life can be messy, and ours is no exception. Along the way there have been broken pieces and intense drama. But despite the mess, we are here; and as long as God continues to preserve us, we will keep getting up, no matter how hard we fall.

My prayer is that as you thumb through these pages you will become inspired to keep fighting, keep hoping, and

Our Journey: By B.J. Bohne

to know that with God's help, nothing – absolutely nothing– is impossible!

– *B.J. Bohne*

Part One:
The Beginning

Chapter 1

The Bohne Family

I never heard my parents say they loved me. We were raised with a strict work ethic, with no sense of entitlement whatsoever.

— Jim Bohne

"So is Grandpa never, ever coming back?"

"Who will play with me now?"

"What is Grandma going to do?"

"Why?"

"Those were the questions that filled my inquisitive five-year-old mind on a chilly May morning in 1975. As I looked through the back window of our home, I longed for my favorite grandpa to return. I wished I could sit on his lap and ride around in his tractor once more. It was not until the paramedics finally wheeled

Our Journey: By B.J. Bohne

his lifeless body away that it really hit me: Grandpa Art was never coming home. – B.J. Bohne

Roots

Arthur A. Bohne was born and raised in Blue Island, Illinois, on a one hundred acre farm where his father, Chicago detective Christian Bohne, and mother raised ten kids: five boys and five girls.

When he passed away, Christian bequeathed the farm to his five boys. During those days, girls didn't really get much of an inheritance. According to German tradition, the girls would marry and be taken care of by their husbands. In reality, this was an ideal way to ensure the husbands - the in-laws - were prevented from taking property away from the family.

Art was both a farmer and a crane operator for the local union, as were his brothers. He married his sweetheart, Mary, at an early age and they immediately started a family. They had four children: two daughters, Jane and Carol and fraternal twins, Jim and John.

Art and Mary both had nine siblings, providing their children with forty uncles and aunties.

Imperial Crane

"Our family get-togethers were massive. My uncles would kill close to one hundred chickens for the meals. Sometimes they slaughtered a whole steer in the basement and sliced it up, leaving the remains for the ladies to make sausages. Remember, we didn't have deep freezers, so preservation was done primitively."
"Within our family we had electricians, farmers, and builders - pretty much everything; and between them, the Bohne's could do practically anything. We had one very self-sustaining community." – Jim Bohne

The Twins

The twins fought all the time. One day, Grandpa Art got completely fed up with all of the hostility and fighting, so he decided to throw them out of the house to sort it out. "Go kill each other out there," he declared; and so, the fighting began. An hour later, they were still going at each other. Grandpa came out and said, "Stop, I can't watch this anymore."

"Sure we fought, but we still had each other's backs. The minute one of us got attacked, we stood up for each other." – Jim Bohne

Interestingly, as B.J. and I read through this story, his face brightened and he began to chuckle.

Our Journey: By B.J. Bohne

*"Dr. Dennis, I find it funny that years later, Dad did exactly the same thing with us when Lance and I would fight. There were no taking sides with him. He'd say, 'I don't care who is right or wrong. You boys take your fight outside, and don't come back until you've figured it out. If you want to kill each other, have at it.'" –
B.J.*

Jim and John were enrolled in First Lutheran Grade School. They rode the bus each morning, but unfortunately, it didn't come down their street. Having to walk a good distance to the nearest stop, they met many other kids from around the neighborhood.

"We had White, Black, and Mexican friends," Jim recalls. "Conversely, we also had White, Black, and Mexican kids who wanted to kill us. Still, nobody dared mess with John and me; we were ferocious fighters."

Being a farmer with five acres of land, Grandpa Art grew onions, tomatoes, sweet corn, and a host of other vegetables. Although Jim and John were officially farm hands, he never gave them any money; he encouraged them to earn it. "If you want money, you've gotta work for it," was his mantra. Living close to two golf courses, Grandpa Art made the boys work as caddies for extra cash, waking them up at 5:00 a.m. to go to work. When they got home, he would assign rows of onions or corn to farm.

Imperial Crane

He even built a little stand in front of the house where they would sell the produce they had worked so hard to grow. The boys would sit there and sell tomatoes for five cents a pound; onions for fifteen cents a pound. Whatever they didn't sell, Grandma Mary would can and store for the family's use, or sometimes to sell in the local market.

Grandpa Art and Grandma Mary valued hard work and diligence, and hastened to instill the same appreciation in their children; especially the boys. Hard work was part of life. You worked, *and then* you played. You worked, *and then* you ate. You worked *in order* to live.

Travel Tip:

All Who Pay the Price of Hard Work Will Reap Its Benefits

It wasn't long after the boys had proven they could handle themselves that Grandpa Art had them working for him on the cranes.

The twins enrolled at *Blue Island High School*, where they played football in Little League and Pony League football. It was there that John met Joan, a beautiful girl with whom he fell madly in love.

"John would drive around with a picture of Joan on the column of his steering wheel; head-over-heels in love with her. In fact, if it weren't for his encounter with

15

Our Journey: By B.J. Bohne

a priest, he would have even left his Lutheran roots and converted to Catholicism to please her. One day he confided in me: "You're not going to believe this, Jim. I went and saw this priest in Orland, and the first thing he did was put his hand on my leg. He then began to tell me how he could satisfy me more than any girl ever could. If there was any chance of me becoming a Catholic, it's gone now!'" – Jim Bohne

Grandpa Art always told his sons that when they turned eighteen, they could do whatever they wanted to: work, go back to school, or stay home. The only stipulation was if their choice involved staying at home, then they could count on paying for their room and board. "Both your sisters worked through school, so it's up to you. Doesn't matter to me," he announced.

"All of us paid our way through school, including the girls. My older sister Carol graduated from Purdue University and moved to Houston. Jane graduated from the University of Colorado. I, too, chose to go to college, and it was not easy. I had no breaks or days off, not even at Christmas."

"When I got back from school, Dad had jobs lined up and waiting for me. That's what he really contributed to my higher education: the opportunity to make money."

Imperial Crane

"As I said, Dad was not one to hand anyone cash. Although, I do remember him giving me one hundred dollars as I left to return to school one day. He said, 'Don't spend this. Put it in your wallet. You must always have something in your wallet in case you need it.'" – *Jim Bohne*

Separate Ways

At nineteen years of age, John married Joan. He was so in love with her; she was the center of his life. He let everyone around him know it, too; he talked to anyone who would listen about just how wonderful she was. He was devoted and faithful to Joan, but unfortunately, that faithfulness was not reciprocated. Sadly, and suddenly, the marriage ended in divorce; the scars of betrayal and rejection remained with John throughout his life.

Instead of going to college, John decided to seize upon a training opportunity in Wausau, Wisconsin in the insurance field. After becoming a certified broker, and a good one at that, he began to demonstrate an innate, bold tenacity that aided in pushing open the doors of opportunity in the insurance industry.

His early days were not exempt from struggle, however. Such was the day he took a substantial premium from a client and invested it in the stock market, expecting a wind-

Our Journey: By B.J. Bohne

fall. Of course, the stock crashed, plunging him into serious debt. Nothing, however, extinguished John's hunger for success. There are defining moments in each of our lives, and John's decision to forego college in favor of an insurance brokerage career brought him to a critical fork in the road to his destiny. Would he let his lack of education define his life? Was he going to settle for a less than average future simply because he lacked a diploma on the wall? On the contrary, John decided he would prove to both himself and his dad that success would not elude him; with or without a college degree.

> *"I believe this decision defined Dad's life. By not having gone to college, he was forced to measure up. Consequently, Dad completely overcompensated in order to achieve more than he or anyone could have imagined. I dare say, if he had received a higher education, with all of its societal privileges, he would not have accomplished nearly as much as he accomplished without one. Had he been stripped of the tenacious drive to succeed on his own merits, you would not be reading this book." – B.J.*

<u>Boys To Men</u>

One day, Grandpa Art announced: "Boys, I gotta tell you something. I want you to listen to me very carefully. You better figure out how to stay away from the army.

Imperial Crane

If you think you're going to go over to that jungle, get your legs blown off and come back expecting me to take care of you, you're crazy. That whole war doesn't make sense to me. I have no idea why we are there. The best advice I can give you is to get married."

Not one to disobey his dad, Jim's first decision upon graduating from Northern Illinois University in 1964 was to marry his sweetheart, Diane.

Travel Tip:

When You Focus On Your Handicaps, You Become Paralyzed With Excuses

Jim and Diane held their lavish wedding later that year at Chicago's Hyatt Park Ridge. While the band played and his fraternity brothers, family, and friends were enjoying the party, Diane's alcoholic father was busy running up an astronomical tab. Consequently, at the end of the festivities, the bill was too large for Diane's family to pay. Without hesitating, John stepped up and put the tab on his new American Express card.

Jim recalls, "I will never forget his generosity that day; and every day. If he had it, and you didn't, there was no question whether or not he would step up. That was my brother John."

Our Journey: By B.J. Bohne

I don't believe in karma, per se, but I do believe in the principle of sowing and reaping. It was right there at Jim's wedding that John's generosity was rewarded by a wonderful gift in the form of a dashing young lady named Gayle.

"He seemed rather dorky to me. He was like an old man; drove this big Cadillac and wore a suit. I thought, 'What is wrong with him?' I could see through the façade. John wasn't rich like he wanted us all to think, but he was an excellent showman with a huge ego; and he knew how to impress the ladies. The only problem was that all his charm and quick wit weren't enough to sway "this" girl; at least that's what I thought." – Gayle Bohne

Gayle was different than all the other girls John had met.

Gayle Nicholas

"We didn't think we were poor, because our parents always told us how precious we were. They always affirmed our gifts and assured us we could do whatever we set our minds to; that if we worked hard enough, we could be anything we wanted to be" – Gayle Bohne

Gayle Nicholas was from exceptional stock – a daughter of Ray T. and Willadene Nicholas, born in Grayslake, Illinois.

Imperial Crane

Grandpa Ray worked as the agricultural agent and horticulturalist for Lake County, Illinois. Grandma Willadene was the family matriarch, who enjoyed a very rich heritage. Her ancestors actually came to the U.S.A. on the Mayflower, while another distant relative was a signer of America's Declaration of Independence.

Grandma Willadene was extremely intelligent, skipping three grades to graduate from Galesburg High School at age sixteen. She studied art and English at the University of Illinois, where Ray would later hold a faculty position. She spent the bulk of her career as a Latin teacher at Stake High School in Wilmette, Illinois.

In the small town of Grayslake, everything seemed to center around the church. Events such as youth group, potluck dinners, and get-togethers all happened in and around the church. Once a week, though, Grandpa Ray and Grandma Willadene took their daughters to the Chicago Arena for ice skating lessons. Eventually, Ray built them an ice skating rink in their own backyard, with music and lights to boot. "I still remember Dad going out to the backyard in the frigid Chicago winters to flood the rink," says Gayle. The skating rink was such a hit with the neighborhood kids; they came over to the Nicolas house to skate every day. Later, Gayle developed a real passion for the sport and ended up becoming a professional ice skater; something that helped pay her way through college.

Our Journey: By B.J. Bohne

A consummate reader, Grandma Willadene loved Shakespeare and almost every type of English poetry; a passion she carried throughout her early years as a home-maker and wife. Being educationists, they made sure they instilled a culture of reading into their children.

> *"Mom wanted each of us to have an excellent vo-cabulary and command of the English language. Bad grammar was simply inexcusable. We had to learn to express ourselves with class and clarity. I often heard her say, 'Gayle dear, instead of wasting time on that paint-by-number set, why don't you pick up a book and read?' When she found me reading a romance novel, she would insist that I feast on the literary wealth of Shakespeare instead." – Gayle Bohne*

Gayle was diagnosed with polio in 1954. The debilitating disease took a considerable toll on her health. Doctors said that the infection had advanced to within a mere eighth of an inch from her brain. Thank God she was able to recover without any significant damage.

The Nicholas family was not rich by any means, but they did have strong values and a high regard for character and constant self-improvement. "Do anything to better yourself," Grandma Willadene always told her girls. It is no wonder then that Gayle played the piano, organ, guitar, ukulele, clarinet, and bass clarinet. She was also an effective debater on the school team, and often led the all-school discussion forums.

Grandma Willadene

Grandma Willadene was clearly one of her student's favorite teachers. At a recent class reunion, for example, Stake High School asked the alumni to name their most influential teacher, and the near unanimous choice was Willadene Nicholas. They particularly noted her passion and care, and how they always knew she wanted the best for them. When she couldn't find a good Latin textbook, she decided to write one so her students would have exactly what they needed. She even opened her home, on her own time, to teach adult art classes and painting lessons.

That same passion for teaching attached itself to Gayle. After graduating from Bradley University in Peoria, she ac-quired a teaching position at Antioch High School. To this day, Bradley University awards the **Gayle Nicholas Bohne Scholarship** to its speech majors – a celebration of a fruitful career.

Grandma Willadene and Grandpa Ray were married for nearly sixty years before he passed away in 1992 from Parkin-son's disease.

Being single again was difficult for Grandma Willadene; sixty years is a long time to share life's journey with someone.

Our Journey: By B.J. Bohne

Instead of pulling back and slowing down, however, Grandma Willadene immersed herself in her writing; publishing a total of eight books, all after her seventieth birthday. Ever the benevolent one, she donated most of the profits from those books to medical research. Grandma Willadene also wrote beautiful, touching poems; a few of which we have the honor of including in this book.

Travel Tip:

After You Have Walked Through The Open Door, Be Sure To Keep It Open For Someone Else

"Grandma Willadene's rich heritage gave me, first and foremost, a sense of confidence. My ancestors were actively involved in the inception of these United States, the greatest nation on the face of the earth. In other words, I am born of a rich heritage and have a place at the proverbial table in this great American experiment."

"This has made me passionate about immigration reform. I am a descendant of immigrants, as are most Americans. It is my belief that we, as a nation, need to continue to make America as welcoming as possible. If our forefathers hadn't come here, we certainly would not be here enjoying this privilege that is America."

Imperial Crane

"Second, Grandma Willadene is largely responsible for my love of art. Every time we visited with her in their beautiful Grayslake home, she would encourage me to draw and paint. I fondly remember those visits, her smile, and gentle demeanor, as if it were yesterday; I'm grateful for those moments" – B.J.

In one of her poems, *Rainbows of Love*, Grandma Willadene wrote:

**Love is a rainbow
For everyone to see
God's special message
He gives to you and me**

This was simply how that special woman, Willadene Nicholas, saw life. She died on August 1, 2007 at the rich age of ninety-seven. The Chicago Tribune, for which she frequently contributed, had this to say:

"Willadene Nicholas had a curious, keen mind and always had a handle on the issues of the day. Hers was a life spent brightening the lives of others through art and poetry."

Chapter Travel Tips

#1: All Who Pay The Price Of Hard Work Will Reap Its Benefits

It wasn't until I understood this principle that I could sympathize with the single father on welfare who wins a $1 million lottery, but after a couple of years ends up in bankruptcy court; or the unsuspecting homeless woman, named heiress to a fortune, who quickly squanders it and is eventually back on welfare. The reason is, these people have been rewarded without having done any real work to merit that reward. The great Thomas Edison said, "Opportunity is missed by most people, because it is dressed in overalls and looks like work. Failure is really a matter of conceit; people don't work hard because, in their conceit, they imagine they will succeed without ever making an effort. Most people believe that they'll wake up someday and find themselves rich. Actually, they've got it half right, because they will eventually wake up."

#2: When You Focus On Your Handicaps, You Become Paralyzed With Excuses

We all have regrets and handicaps life has thrown at us: the abusive upbringing, the negligent parents, or the economic dilapidation. We wish we were born somewhere else, or in another family, or with better looks or skills. Try as we might, we cannot change our history; but we can certainly rewrite our future.

Our Journey: By B.J. Bohne

#3: After You Have Walked Through The Open Door, Be Sure To Keep It Open For Someone Else

It is always unfortunate when we fail to take notice of life's privileges and opportunities: the open doors. It is even more tragic when we hasten to shut the open doors after we walk through them. As you journey, keep in mind that someone else is walking behind you. They will need the same opportunity you have enjoyed. Be sure to keep that door open after you have walked through it.

Somewhere A Child

Somewhere a child is laughing –
Somewhere a lover sighs.
Somewhere children are playing –
Somewhere a mother cries.

Somewhere a loved one listens
For your footstep at the door
Somewhere a dewdrop glistens
And a rose is refreshed once more.

Somewhere people are praying
For a new beginning everywhere.
Somewhere the sun is shining
On a desert bleak and bare.

Somewhere comes understanding
And an enemy is soon a friend.
Somewhere a life is beginning
But where does a rainbow end?

Willadene
"The Master's Treasures"
Copyright 2000

"Before I formed you in the womb I knew you, before you were born I set you apart."

Jeremiah 1:5 (NIV)

Chapter 2

The Bohne Home

I always thought, "Look around you B.J., there is a reason why all the kids want to hang out here. Yup . . . your mom is the best!"

– B.J. Bohne

Gayle was charmingly beautiful, right down to the way she walked, talked, and carried herself.

> *"I remember the first time John showed up with Gayle. Boy was she hot! The guys couldn't take their eyes off of her! John knew it too, and was not about to let this one go. He would make the ninety-minute drive every night from Blue Island to Grayslake to see her. Quite often, he'd stay overnight in one of the spare rooms in her parent's home, only to be awake at the crack of dawn, ready to drive back to work." – Larry Gedmin, long time friend and business associate.*

> *"One day, John showed up to take me skiing at Wilmette. Although it was my favorite sport, he wasn't a*

Our Journey: By B.J. Bohne

skier at all. He didn't let that stop him, though, from buying me a brand new set of skis. To me, this was a big deal."

"On my $5,400 annual teacher's salary, this represented a year's worth of saving. Plainly, he was splurging to impress me, and although I was flattered, it made me mad, somehow, that he could spend so much money, even on me." – Gayle Bohne

On June 21, 1968, John and Gayle were married in Grandma Willadene's rose garden.

A Young Family

After their honeymoon, and having settled into a small apartment in Crestwood, Illinois, John returned to his day job as an insurance agent, while also moonlighting as a crane operator for Canon Steel Erection. Though she had her own full-time teaching job, Gayle found time to help her new husband write up insurance premiums for his clients.

A little more than one year after the wedding, on August 12, 1969, their first-born, Lancelot Arthur, arrived. He is named after the ancient literary character Sir Lancelot, something Gayle's family didn't find amusing at all. As erudite as they were, they had hoped for a name with greater meaning or

Imperial Crane

significance. Lance's birth brought new responsibilities and pressures to the relatively young couple.

Like most dads, John wasn't really ready to be a father, having not yet anticipated the intrusion babyhood would bring. He didn't care for the constant diaper changing, the crying, the sleepless nights, or the unremitting attention that came with the new addition. In short, he had major adjustment issues that started to stress their fledgling relationship.

Consequently, Gayle moved to the basement with baby Lance in an effort to reduce the tension, as John continued to bury himself in his work. He had a company to build, and nothing was going to get in his way.

Gayle took only one month off for her maternity leave, so she could get right back to work and continue earning her much needed salary. While she worked, she dropped Lance off with various babysitters in all kinds of inclement Chicago weather.

As she was beginning to recover from the birth and was finally getting some kind of rhythm back into her life, Gayle realized she was pregnant again. Although welcome, the news was somewhat unexpected. With John working two jobs and with her still teaching, life, as they knew it, was about to drastically change.

Our Journey: By B.J. Bohne

"Being nine months pregnant with a one-year-old pulling on your apron strings can be physically challenging for any mother. I needed help. With John gone, I would make the one hour drive out to my parent's home in Grayslake so I at least had someone with me when the big moment arrived. I still remember that big moment like it was yesterday; it was on Lance's first birthday when I went into labor."

"Come to think of it, had it not been for the long drive to Waukegan, the boys might have easily shared the same birthday."   *–Gayle Bohne*

On August 13, 1970, Berkshire John Bohne was born at St. Theresa Hospital in Waukegan, Illinois. Fancy name, Berkshire. Perhaps even aristocratic; but John Bohne wasn't about to give his kid a common name.

Mere days after Gayle and her newborn were discharged from the hospital, she started hemorrhaging heavily. Although she was immediately readmitted, she very nearly lost her life due to major complications, and was completely bedridden for the next few months.

As a result of these difficulties, she was unable to hold her new baby boy, nurture him or provide the critical infant care only a mother can give.

Imperial Crane

Thank God for her grandmother Eda, who had the time to nurture baby B.J. and help care for young Lance while she recovered.

Thinking about those fragile early days of his life, B.J. pondered the grace of God. He could have died at birth. His mother could have died while delivering him. By every indication, his arrival was not an easy one. Although, in hindsight, he believes that God had him in mind the whole time.

Travel Tip:

You Are Not Here By Accident. Before You Were Born, God Knew All About You

"It was forty years later when I began to see God's master plan in my life. I had accompanied Dr. Dennis on a mission trip to Guatemala where a gentleman I had never met walked up to me and said, 'Sir, I traveled three days by bus from Mexico City to attend this conference. I know that one of the main reasons I am here is to give you a special word from God, and here it is: "The devil has tried to destroy you, but the hand of God is upon you. You are going to impact many people because it's your destiny." For over five minutes, this stranger spoke many astonishingly accurate truths concerning my life; things only I knew. I was completely blown away, while at the same time deeply touched and

Our Journey: By B.J. Bohne

inspired. The experience marked my life and made me remember my difficult birth. Indeed, I could have died. Perhaps it is true that God knew my journey before it even began; that God really knew about B.J. long before he was born. I still have that now furrowed piece of paper on which I wrote the gentleman's words. Every so often I look at it, and remember God's goodness to me. No, I am definitely not an accident!" –B.J.

The doctor botched B.J.'s birth so badly that many medical experts feared Gayle would never have any more children. They were wrong; twelve years later, she would give birth to another beautiful son, Jonathan.

Hard Lessons

Grandpa Art and Grandma Mary decided to invite John, Gayle, and the boys to move in with them in Palos Heights, Illinois, figuring Gayle could use the extra help with her growing family. Selflessly, Art and Mary moved into the smaller guesthouse on the property and left the main house to the young family.

It was a modest home with two bedrooms: one for the boys, and the other for John and Gayle. They all shared one bathroom and had bitter fights about that. Though they didn't have much money, they had each other; they had

Imperial Crane

meals together, played together and grew together, even as John continued to work long hours on his two jobs.

"Dad, someone just stole by bike," four-year-old B.J. cried.

"So what?" John asked firmly.

• • •

Travel Tip:

Sometimes Life Isn't Fair; It's Pointless Trying To Understand All Its Curveballs

"Well, I want a new one. Please, Dad, aren't you going to buy me another one? It wasn't my fault, you know. It was right here in the front yard, and now it's gone."

B.J. didn't get a new bike, and for days he mourned the loss. At this tender age, life was teaching him a pivotal lesson: sometimes bad things happen that you cannot remedy or fix.

• • •

Sometimes, you will lose things you will never get back, however hard you try. Today, he is thankful his parents didn't replace his bicycle.

The Bohne's grew up Lutheran. Unlike John, Gayle was an avid churchgoer. During the summer, she would drive the kids and their friends to their summer cottage in Land-o-

Our Journey: By B.J. Bohne

Lakes, Wisconsin. They would hang out at the local church, where they would play games with the local kids.

Wednesday was bingo night at the church town hall, and this particular Wednesday started out the same as most others. There must have been three hundred people there including Gayle, the boys, and one of their friends. Settling into their seats, Gayle handed out the bingo cards she bought: one for each of the three boys, and twenty for herself.

• • •

Travel Tip:

**Play The
Hand You
Have Been
Dealt;
Never Mind
The Odds
Against You**

As the numbers were called, Gayle repeated the ones that were on her cards, "B-3. O-6." She was on a roll. B.J. quickly saw the inequity occurring and complained, "Mom, this isn't fair! You have twenty chances to win. We only have one chance each."

• • •

At first, Gayle tried to quiet him. "Stop whining, B.J. Just keep playing." But he wouldn't quit. Out of frustration, she took her twenty bingo cards and gave them all to B.J. "There! Give me your card. Now, let's play!"

B.J. looked at all of the cards and was thrilled, anticipating his imminent victory. That was until, moments later, Gayle

Imperial Crane

cried out, "BINGO!" She won the game and $300, with B.J.'s lone bingo card. B.J. was excited that they won, especially since they won with his card; he quickly calculated his share of the take. "Mom! We won! We won!" he shouted. Gayle turned to her son and said, "What? What are you talking about? You didn't win, I did!" B.J. was devastated. He still remembers that moment to this day. He also remembers the lesson he learned: To win, you need to focus on playing your own hand the very best you can. Stop wishing you had someone else's hand.

B.J. didn't know it at the time, but it was a good thing his mom won the money. As it turned out, Gayle was running low on cash; with John so far away, she was up against a wall financially, and $300 was exactly what she needed to buy groceries and take care of the family for the next few days.

A Cool Mom

John continued to work many late hours, but at least once a month he made time to take the family to Dunlap's, the same local steakhouse where, as a child, he had worked as a busboy stuffing olives with anchovies.

"Dad was always away working. I didn't resent him for it; I understood he had to provide for us. In fact, I actually wanted to be like him: a hard worker and a

Our Journey: By B.J. Bohne

great provider. One aspect to him not being home much was that there was a lot of Mom around. She was the matriarch of the family, and boy was she amazing! In fact, she was wonderful and I'm confident there was no doubt in anyone's mind about who had the coolest mom in the neighborhood; it was us. Our mother, Gayle Bohne!" – B.J.

"Dad influenced us a lot. He was the disciplinarian and we were afraid of displeasing him. Whatever we did, we did not want to get on his bad side. He had a scary demeanor, but if you got to know him, he was more like a big puppy dog than anything. He had a big heart and if you knew him, he became your favorite person. Unfortunately, he was hardly home so we all leaned on Mom – a lot. She did a great deal to keep everything in order." – Lance

Years later, at a special tribute organized by one of her classes, everyone got to see how much Gayle had impacted lives outside of her home. Corporate heads, doctors, managers, celebrities, and grateful students from all walks of life gathered together to pay tribute to Gayle.

One Northwestern University law professor testified that for years she had endured sexual abuse from her father. She said had it not been for those precious hours after school

Imperial Crane

spent at Mrs. Gayle Bohne's house, she would not have survived.

Through the pregnancies and John's early business ups and downs, she didn't take anything for granted. Even when John started making money, she kept her part-time job as a substitute teacher for Antioch High School. She valued whatever little amount of money she had; even the twenty dollars in her pocket. "Hey, you never know when it'll come in handy!"

> "Mom was always there to drop us off and pick us up from school. She did class projects with us and never allowed us to feel Dad's absence. I remember her buying some really expensive picture frames for our drawings and paintings. No matter how ugly they may have looked, she treated them like masterpieces. We never heard Mom say, 'We cannot afford this.' She constantly told us how wonderful we were; that we could become whatever we wanted to become. She also taught us kindness. 'Always show respect to people,' she would say, 'no matter who they are. That older man could be Grandpa Ray or Grandma Mary'." – B.J.

> "My earliest memories were pleasant. Mom did a lot to keep everything in order. I remember Dad being gone, but when he was there, we had lots of fun.

Our Journey: By B.J. Bohne

Whether it was riding motorcycles up in Wisconsin or riding Grandpa Art's tractor, we were into everything. We were boys. All in all, I had a blessed childhood with family around me as far back as I can remember." – Lance

"I was sitting at home one night preparing to start high school the following day when John called to offer me a job. I told him I had a job washing dishes at Dunlap Restaurant that paid me a handsome twenty-five dollars a week. 'Well, you are family,' he said. 'You gotta come work for me. I'll pick you up first thing tomorrow morning.' I had school, and besides, I really didn't know him that well. And what about the money? My dad encouraged me to ask him directly. 'I guarantee you thirty dollars a week, whether you work or not. Guaranteed,' John emphasized. That was a deal I could not turn down. In 1974, that was a huge amount of money."

"Every Saturday after that, I'd be at the house at 8:00 a.m. I'd do anything he wanted me to: wash Gayle's car, baby-sit Lance and B.J., whatever! Then, we'd follow John's Saturday morning ritual: I'd drive him out for breakfast with his buddies, and then I'd take him to the bank after which I'd drive him back to the office to read his mail. After that, I'd drive him to Far Away Joe's, his favorite pizza joint, for lunch. John became

Imperial Crane

like a father to me. When I had a hot date, he'd even let me use Gayle's Cadillac." – Rick Bohne, B.J.'s third cousin

On May 11, 1975, Grandpa Art passed away from a sudden heart attack. Fearing how John would take the news, Gayle had the boys tell him. After the funeral and burial arrangements were completed, B.J. asked Gayle, "Mom, may I go stay with Grandma? She's all alone now, with Grandpa gone."

Gayle agreed. And every night, young B.J. made the one hundred yard dash across the back yard to Grandma Mary's house in order to keep her company.

"I wanted to comfort her and maybe make some of her pain go away. As a result, she grew really fond of me and we spent a lot of time together. She loved me and made absolutely no bones about it. In fact, there was no mistaking which of us was her favorite."

"When Lance and I got into a fight, guess who was always on my side? Grandma Mary. As far as she was concerned, I was always in the right. Ours is a relationship I truly miss." – B.J.

As she grew older, Grandma Mary needed more and more help getting around and taking care of herself. Con-

Our Journey: By B.J. Bohne

sequently, Jim hired a wonderful Polish lady who helped Gayle take care of her for the remainder of her life. Sadly, Grandma Mary passed away on November 13, 1992.

With his mom and dad now gone, John eventually purchased their five-acre home and built a new house on the property.

That Thing Called Work

One summer, Gayle decided to send the kids to her sister Sally's farm in Dodgeville, Wisconsin. After two days, Lance decided he wanted to come home.

"Mom, come get me," he pleaded.

"Are you not having fun with Aunt Sally? Well sure, I'll be right there," Gayle replied. She promptly drove out to get the boys, but discovered that B.J. wanted to stay. In fact, he stayed through the whole summer, enjoying rodeos and competing in barrel races. Life on Aunt Sally's farm was not all fun and games, however.

Early each morning when the roosters started crowing, it was time to get up, even though everything inside of him wanted to stay right there in bed. He had work to do, excrement to shovel, and animals to feed. Sally had him work her horse shows in the heat of summer.

Imperial Crane

"It was on that farm where I was introduced to sacrifice. I learned there are things in life that have to be done, whether or not I enjoy doing them. I learned there that life doesn't revolve around B.J. or what B.J. wants to do. I learned the heart of discipline."

"Later in life, when duty called, I knew I had to answer whether it was comfortable or not. It was then that I would draw on those simple lessons I learned at Aunt Sally's."
– B.J.

Travel Tip:

Hard Work Is the Price You Pay For Success

That trip afforded him a critical life-lesson that he embraces to this day: diligence and hard work pay dividends in the form of success and fulfillment.

"Today, there are countless things I don't necessarily enjoy doing, but I do them nonetheless. For example, I recently had a very late-night dinner meeting with a potential client."

"Frankly, I would have rather spent the evening at home with my girls than with someone I hardly knew. But my sense of duty dictated my priorities. This is something I did, and actually enjoyed, not because I was forced to, but because of my work ethic."

Our Journey: By B.J. Bohne

"As the head of a large corporation, I am fully aware that hundreds of families depend on me to make certain sacrifices, and I am happy to pay the price leadership so often demands of me." – B.J.

Finding B.J.

"Debate clubs, drama clubs, sports teams, and extra-curricular activities were of no real interest to me. I was curious about money, success, and power. While my classmates partied and went clubbing after school, I worked with Dad on the cranes. Somehow, I honestly thought work was a much better investment of my time."

"For me, the path was clear; the choice was simple. While others were looking to find themselves, I had my distraction: the crane business." – B.J.

That's not to say he didn't have fun.

With the notoriety that came with a name like B.J. Bohne, one can only imagine the impression he left amongst his peers; especially the ladies.

"When we threw a party, modesty wasn't our goal. Literally hundreds would come, and boy did we drink and dance the night away." – B.J.

Imperial Crane

With such popularity, a well-to-do family and solid social standing, one would think B.J. had scores of friends. He didn't.

> "As early as I can remember, I was not a follower. I didn't do things simply because everyone else was doing them. Whatever it was, I did it because I was into it at the time. When I was done with it, it was game over, regardless who else was still doing it. 'I set trends, I don't follow them,' was my mantra." – B.J.

That attitude perhaps seems cocky or arrogant, but it may have saved B.J. from the dangerous tides of youthful peer pressure. When his buddies were skipping class, or were partying to no end, he wanted to work and excel. Was he a born leader? Perhaps. But whatever the case, being around his father and the demanding work environment helped him keep his head on straight.

> "I remember wanting to hang out with my old man. I'd ask to go places with him, even when I knew I'd probably be bored. He would say, 'Well, I'm not sure you'll have fun here, but yeah, sure, c'mon.' He'd tell me to meet him at a particular restaurant or to jump into the back seat and we'd ride together. He never turned me away. Sometimes, I would even go with him and his buddies for whole weekend excursions to our summer home. They'd be drinking, smoking cigars and

Our Journey: By B.J. Bohne

talking business while I played video games and watched TV. It certainly wasn't an ideal environment for a kid, but it presented an opportunity for me to listen to grown-up talk for hours on end. I heard my father's philosophies on work, politics, unions, competition, women, and so on. Undoubtedly, it impacted me more than I realized then, and I'm certain that some of the things I do today, unintentionally mimicking my dad's behavior, are a result of those moments." – B.J.

By the 1980s, John's climb up the economic ladder started to gain serious traction. The young boys had begun enjoying the privileged life: limousine rides to school, concerts, shows, sporting events, and parties all became commonplace.

While life on the surface seemed pleasant and considerably comfortable, there were many things about their father they didn't understand: the curious absences, the late-night steak dinners, golfing excursions, and the long business trips.

"John didn't spend much time with his kids; he was busy building the business. We would take clients golfing, to play tennis, and away on weekend excursions. In fact, I remember spending most Februarys in Acapulco, away from the family." –Jim Bohne

Chapter Travel Tips

#4: You Are Not Here By Accident. Before You Were Born, God Knew All About You

Your genetic composition; your fingertips, blood type, chemistry, eye color, and skin shade all make for a very unique and special human being – YOU! God, who made you, does not do things haphazardly. He is deliberate. It is not by some roll of the dice that you were formed the way you were. The Psalmist wrote: "Thank you for making me so wonderfully complex! Your workmanship is marvelous; and how well I know it." (Psalm 139:14 NLT) You are special!

#5: Sometimes Life Isn't Fair; It's Pointless Trying To Understand All Its Curveballs

As you journey through life, you will experience losses; sometimes big losses. Your loved ones will not always be there to insulate you from life's harsh curveballs or help you replace lost gains. It is then that you are given a gift; a gift given along with a pivotal choice. Will you keep asking why, sulk, and look for someone to blame, or will you get up, pick up the pieces and journey on to the next season of your life?

Our Journey: By B.J. Bohne

#6: Play The Hand You Have Been Dealt; Never Mind The Odds Against You

We don't get to choose where we are born, our skin color, or our parentage. Quite simply, we cannot rewrite history or change a single whisper of our yesterdays. It is how we choose to respond to our circumstances that determines the very outcome of our lives. The English have a proverb that says, "Every man must row with the oars he has been given."

#7: Hard Work Is The Price You Pay For Success

The Bible says, "Good planning and hard work lead to prosperity, but hasty shortcuts lead to poverty" (Proverbs 21:5 NLT). Everyone we may call an overnight success has spent years in private preparation. Simply having a dream or desire is not enough. You have to roll up your sleeves and become diligent in what God has given you to do. Get a job. Stay on the job. Work the job. Do something with your hands, and do it well; and long enough to count. Then you will begin to enjoy success. The great sculptor Michelangelo said, "If people knew how hard I had to work to gain my mastery, it wouldn't seem wonderful at all."

Lancelot Arthur

Lancelot Arthur – born with princely charm –
Such a beautiful child at once endears.
Your deep brown eyes hold all entranced
By inner perception beyond your years

A born leader at once we see
Beloved by all ages we'll all agree.
Restrained and calm through troubled times,
Yet alert for action when the right bell chimes

Lancelot Arthur – our little prince,
In your brown eyes of wisdom of sages
Passed down through your ancestors
With honor and courage and the Truth of the ages

Your kingdom throughout the world extends
As for all little children the future portends
Vast sunny blue skies for happiness cast
And bestowed by the love of those in your past

I remember when we cut your baby curls –
I see your puckered lips as your mother sighs.
And your cute little nose – but most of all
I remember the vast depths of your beautiful brown eyes

It seems you carried along from ages past
The mysteries of life so vast.
How much you knew even then
Of Truths that baffled other men

You played all the children's little games;
You lived your childhood just like others
But your eyes reflect the highest aims,
For the living of life as the Lord acclaims

B.J. Bohne

Little artist boy, our B.J.
So gifted with your brush and pen,
So like a man while still a child,
So rugged yet so tender then.

I think of you with your bloody nose
As you convinced your brother
That you had muscles, as you arose
From a losing battle to fight another.

Your talent to see all the colors of the rainbow,
To cherish your family, friends, and home.
To appreciate all living things
Is in each painting like a poem.

You planted a little garden –
You were exuberant when it grew.
You watered the parched flowers
And pulled a weed or two.

You helped your grandma with a chore –
You painted pictures really fine.
You stood up strong when the need arose –
You held perspective with a line.

You knew the habits of the bees.
The great outdoors was your domain,
And even after getting stung
Your zest for living subdued the pain.

Our Journey: By B.J. Bohne

Now B.J., you're growing up so fast
And can do with skill so many things –
With your zest for life and love for all
You're prepared for whatever the future brings

Willadene
"A Child Can Dream and other Poems and Prose"
Copyright 1981

"Judge not, that you be not judged. For with what judgment you judge, you will be judged; and with the measure you use, it will be measured back to you. And why do you look at the speck in your brother's eye, but do not consider the plank in your own eye? Or how can you say to your brother, 'Let me remove the speck from your eye'; and look, a plank is in your own eye? Hypocrite! First remove the plank from your own eye, and then you will see clearly to remove the speck from your brother's eye."

Matthew 7:1-5 (NKJV)

Chapter Three:

The Bohne Boys

"John was always frustrated with his boys. Yeah, he loved them, but boy were they a sore subject! He fired and rehired them many times over."

– Jeff Bohne

Even while the rest of the USA was burdened with the fear of an imminent Russian nuclear attack, John was enjoying the fast life; the huge sums of money and subsequent power that come with financial success.

Marist

John learned that most of his Chicago bigwig buddies had their kids in private Catholic high schools. They figured the structure and general religious ethic would serve well to protect them from negative societal influences.

Immediately, he enrolled Lance and B.J. into Marist High School, a private Catholic school with over two thousand students, in Alsip, Illinois.

Our Journey: By B.J. Bohne

"School life had been pretty mundane. We went to school and came home; did our homework, maybe played a game and went to bed. It was uneventful until Dad took us to Marist; that was different. Though strict, it was a great school with high standards. In fact, when I got to college, school work seemed like a piece of cake because I had become used to Marist's high academic standards." – Lance

The Bohne boys had no clue about Catholicism, having being raised Lutheran. So when their peers discussed the Catholic sacraments or prayed the rosary, B.J. and Lance were clueless. "We faked it; just went through the motions," says B.J. But they quickly adapted, nonetheless.

Unbeknownst to their parents, lurking underneath the strict disciplinarian ethos, preppy school uniforms, and religious camouflage were some of the most unruly elements you would ever want around your children. Right there on campus was an elaborate drug ring run by the notorious John Kappis, famously dubbed Chicago's twenty-two-year-old cocaine drug dealer.

"Mom and Dad sent us to Marist to try and protect us, but ironically it was there we got exposed to the worst peer pressure. I saw drug deals going down right there on campus. I remember one drug related double suicide that literally paralyzed the whole community; it

Imperial Crane

really hit home for the school because we all knew the kids. They were good kids caught up in a dangerous web of cocaine and other hard drugs. All this hit very close to home for me when I began to see my own brother being lured into that pit of addiction." – B.J.

Lance was the typical big brother who found some pleasure in teasing and poking fun of his kid brother once in a while. Unable to run to his parents, B.J. learned to channel his frustration inward. "I learned how to talk to myself, to calm myself and to endure isolation," he says. Despite the sibling tension, B.J. loved and admired Lance a great deal. It was very difficult for him to see his brother struggling.

"I knew very well that I wasn't any better than Lance; I had made some very stupid mistakes myself. I wasn't impervious to the destructive peer pressure we all felt at Marist. But watching Lance's struggles helped me see what could become of those choices. My future was right in front of me if I made the same decisions. I could clearly see how not to act. But I think the reason for my restraint was bigger than mere prudence or discipline; I think it was God who opened my eyes. In fact, and I say this with a measure of sad irony, I owe my life to my brother Lance. Watching him struggle with this firsthand helped me stay away from it. I also found it curious that I had never once met a real user or addict who told me, 'B.J., cocaine is awesome.'

Our Journey: By B.J. Bohne

Even as they were snorting, they would say, 'Buddy, the buzz is cool, but do yourself a favor, stay away. I wish I never did this. It's a disaster.'" – B.J.

<u>Wake-Up Call?</u>

Jonathan Bohne was born on December 24, 1982. His arrival really challenged John. Deep inside, he seemed to know life was giving him another chance to be a better father. Thus, John was noticeably more loving and expressive with Jonathan. In his words, Jonathan declares, "Without a doubt, I think I had the best dad in the world."

"Jonathan would call him for anything. Their relationship was much different than we all had with our dads. For example, while we would often have to go around in circles asking our parents for a sleepover with friends, Jonathan would simply pick up the phone and say, 'Hey Dad, I am sleeping over at Fred's house, okay?' Or he would say, 'Dad, I need four tickets to the Sox game, okay? Okay, bye!" The next call would be telling us where to go to pick the tickets up. You could tell they were close, but not real deep. John was pretty busy all the time and so communication between them seemed short and concise." – Fred Hunssinger, childhood friend and Imperial Crane's Safety Director

Imperial Crane

"John was never demonstrative with B.J. or Lance, but with Jonathan he was very different, showering affection all over him; Gayle did too. I remember when she approached me to help him with a school play. He was good; he could have become an actor if he wanted to. At any rate, John was softer and more affectionate with Jonathan than with the other two boys; clearly a sign of his maturing predilection toward child rearing. I'm sure he would have made a great grandfather." – Pat Walsh, one of John's closest friends

"John had the first two boys during his times of intense struggle; and while he cared for his family, those struggles forced him to ensure he was also looking out for himself. By the time Jonathan was born, he and his circumstances had changed. I am sure he had some regrets with how he raised B.J. and Lance, and saw an opportunity to change that with Jonathan. He showered Jonathan with affection and clearly wanted to be for him what he hadn't been for the others." – Jeff Bohne

This may explain Jonathan's laid back attitude toward work today, but make no mistake; Jonathan is a smart and extremely creative guy.

"I remember giving him ten dollars to wash my car while I was working out at a gym one morning. He was

Our Journey: By B.J. Bohne

excited. An hour later, I came back to find some strange kid washing my car. I asked him who he was, and he said, 'Sir, Jonathan gave me five dollars to wash your car.' I walked into the house and there was Jonathan watching a movie. I thought: genius! I was actually impressed. Here was my kid brother brokering deals at seven years old!" – B.J.

With the way he was treating Jonathan, John was clearly demonstrating he was becoming more aware of his previous bad choices, and seemed to work harder to protect his boys from those earlier, less favorable decisions. For the first time, John Bohne seemed soft and even vulnerable.

"I came in right as the business was starting to explode. Being his driver, I was often the third wheel as he ran around, and as a result, I really got to enjoy the fast life with John. Frankly, I found myself in places I probably shouldn't have been. Any kid my age would have given anything to be in my shoes. I grew up fast. I remember going to him after I graduated high school; my world had just crashed after learning that my parents couldn't afford to send me to college. I'll never forget what he told me: 'Ricky, you don't have to go to college to succeed. You are enrolled into John Bohne College. You have a place here!' He taught me how to budget, how to prepare for the unexpected and much more. John came through on

Imperial Crane

that promise time and time again, bailing me out of many sticky situations as he helped me navigate through life." – Rick Bohne

Searching

"Look, these are my boys. They are coming to work with me and they need permits," demanded John to the local union boss. Although they were definitely underage, B.J. and Lance were issued crane-operating licenses; no questions asked.

"The boys had everything they could ever want. As soon as they broke from school for the summer, John would call and have me schedule them for work. I would line them up on jobs close to their house so they wouldn't be late. I tried to be lenient, but he hated it when they slacked off for any reason. And based on what I saw, I think he was right. I still wonder if they sometimes paid off the operators and snuck out or took off early." – John Tierney, Imperial Crane Dispatcher

While he had an open door with his father with plenty of opportunities for success, B.J. felt a need to explore other interests as well. For a month, he volunteered to go down to Aspen, Colorado to help renovate some apartments with a long time family friend and contractor, John Ziola. John,

Our Journey: By B.J. Bohne

a.k.a. Zeke, still works with B.J. to this day. An incredible support to the family through the years, he still checks up on him at least once a month. Zeke taught him about the carpentry business, but most importantly, he taught him about life and about working with his hands.

After he returned home, the athletic B.J. decided to try modeling. One of Gayle's friends who owned a modeling agency hired him immediately. When he was not operating cranes, B.J. was taking auditions and working on his modeling career. Before long, he landed a few high profile gigs, his face plastered on AT&T billboards up and down the streets of Chicago, as well as on various Pringles products.

John started to recognize B.J. was maturing and seeking his own identity.

"I remember Dad taking me to dinner; just the two of us. That was different. I really enjoyed it. He would buy steaks and expensive wines. In fact, he introduced me to the world of fine wines such as Chateau Le Fit and Silver Oak, which is still my favorite. He would tell me about his mistakes, even his indiscretions. Dad let me see both his strengths and vulnerabilities. One of my childhood highlights was a trip we took to Africa. The two of us enjoyed ten days of safari in Tanzania, hunting game and taking in the wild. On our way back, we stopped over in Paris and lavished at the presidential

Imperial Crane

suite in the luxurious Ritz Carlton, just in time for my six-teenth birthday. These are treasured moments I will never forget. That trip marked my life." – B.J.

"I still regret not going to Africa with my dad. We were both supposed to go. I was seventeen and a lot was going on with me; I was really searching. But I sure wish I had gone. It was one of those once-in-a-lifetime things I missed out on. Although we did go on several overseas trips together after that, it wasn't the same." – Lance

Mixed Messages

"It was my high school graduation, and I was looking for my family. I couldn't see them. Where were they? Finally I saw Mom, alone, and way up in the bleachers. I remember wondering where Dad was. Of course, Mom covered for him, as always; I chose not to think about it." – B.J.

John wasn't at B.J.'s high school graduation because he was playing a big stakes round of golf with his buddy, Coach Mike Ditka, at Bob O'Link Golf Course in Highland Park, Illinois. He hoped to make it out in time for B.J.'s graduation, but couldn't.

Our Journey: By B.J. Bohne

"As I was changing into my trunks to go hang out with my buddies by the pool after graduation, in came Dad, breathless from the frantic rush. He couldn't even enunciate an apology. I actually felt bad for him, maybe even flattered that he was so visibly upset by it. I simply told him, 'Don't worry about it Dad. Glad you're here.'"

"Indeed, I was genuinely glad, but I had another hidden reason for my calm attitude: I finally had something on my old man. Here was one of the most important days of my school life and he'd missed it. I remember saying, 'Dad, it's you and your cronies who wanted me to go to this school, and you don't even show up for my graduation?'" – B.J.

Later in life, when John tried to claim he was there, Gayle pulled out B.J.'s high school yearbook, and there she was: in the bleachers, alone. Over the next twenty years, when John chided him for irresponsibility, B.J. referenced this incident at least two dozen times. And it worked.

"Interestingly, I never heard Mom complain about it; not to me, anyway. My mother always believed that whatever issues they had were their issues, not ours. That stuff was to remain between them, we didn't need to get involved or be forced to choose sides." – B.J.

Imperial Crane

What I find very interesting is that during our interview, Gayle never bashed John in any way. She isn't sure she did all the right things - none of us are - but she did the best she could. Did she overprotect John, and perhaps let him get away with too much? Maybe; and many others believe so as well.

- - -

Travel Tip:

Do Not Put Kids In The Middle of A Grownup Fight

"One of my duties right after John hired me was to take the boys to White Sox games. This meant providing a cover for John to go off and fool around away from Gayle. Although I greatly respected him, and he knew it, this was one area where we had some very heated arguments." – Bill Tierney, Imperial Crane Vice President

Was Gayle a victim of John's hidden pain and insecurities? Perhaps.

- - -

"I think I am a good mother, never mind my failures. My kids meant everything to me. I practically did their homework, their school projects; protected them and nurtured them. I did everything. Like any mother, I never wanted them to suffer or exert themselves. Maybe I was too much of an enabler. Yeah, maybe that is my biggest regret. I enabled Lance, even Jonathan, but not B.J. For sure, I enabled

Our Journey: By B.J. Bohne

John. I still remember him saying to me, 'Gayle, you are a better mother than you are a wife!'" – Gayle Bohne

Whatever you might think of women like Gayle is entirely your prerogative. All over the world, there are courageous women who will do anything to protect their children. For Gayle, nurturing and raising her boys meant suspending her needs and overlooking what most would consider unthinkable; and for that, she will be forever celebrated.

To ASU

"I was sitting up in my room one January morning, a high school sophomore thumbing through a catalogue with different college options. Right at the beginning, under "A", was Arizona State University. My interest was piqued. I loved Arizona, and I loved ASU. My cousin was a freshman there, and had only great things to say about it. Immediately, my eyes went straight to the words, "MEDIAN TEMPERATURE – 82.5 DEGREES, 315 DAYS OF THE YEAR. TOTAL ENROLLMENT 50,000." That was it! 'What's not to like?' I thought. Beautiful weather, gorgeous girls: paradise! 'I am going to Arizona State University,' I declared." – B.J.

In 1988, B.J. decided to move to Arizona. Only one year earlier, Lance had enrolled there. Eventually, his father would

Imperial Crane

buy a house there, and twelve years later Jonathan would also go to Arizona State University.

"Going to ASU was hard for me initially. I virtually lost all my friends; everything was new. Initially, I started out with business as my major, and then switched to sociology. Sometimes friends ask me if I think I wasted time going to school for something I don't even do today."

"I tell them that I still believe it was good for me to get a good education; to be trained in a specialized field of study. I learned a lot at ASU. For me, I proved to myself I could actually start and finish something." – Lance

B.J. still remembers the morning of his departure from Chicago. As he packed his belongings into his GMC Jimmy Blazer, ready for the two thousand mile drive, he felt a rush of emotions. Excited as he was to go, he was sad to leave home.

"To this day I don't know where Mom and Dad were, but guess who was there? Grandma Mary. I remember her pleas: 'Don't leave, B.J. Please stay. I don't want you to go.' I tried to comfort her and assure her I would write often. My heart broke to leave her. We had developed a really tight bond; that was the hardest separation." – B.J.

Our Journey: By B.J. Bohne

B.J. transplanted to Arizona and moved in with his cousin Jeff. The two did everything together; Jeff protected him, loved him and taught him a lot. Although they had been close cousins over the years, their time at ASU helped to form a brotherly bond that continues to this day. Jeff was glad to be there for his cousin; he knew firsthand what it was like to dodge the bullet of peer pressure.

> *"I remember when my son Jeff was having issues at school. In fact, he had inadvertently burned down his teacher's house. He was seriously spiraling and I was very worried. When I asked John for ideas, he said, 'Culvers Military School, Jim. Take him there. He will straighten out for you.' I responded, 'John, it's expensive.' 'Well, it's up to you Jim,' he replied. 'One thing's for sure, it would be a lot cheaper than attorney's fees and rehab. You take the limo and drop him off. He is going to call you everyday to pick him up, but don't.' I took his advice and enrolled him. For weeks, Jeff did call me whining and asking to come get him, but I never budged. He started liking it and eventually fell in love with it. He did very well, graduating with flying colors. That one decision made a difference in my son's life." – Jim Bohne*

From our conversations, its obvious B.J. and Jeff are still very close. They have traveled together and continually work to build Imperial Crane with the rest of the team. In

Imperial Crane

fact, because he lives ninety minutes out of town, every so often, Jeff makes a makeshift residence of B.J.'s guesthouse in Oakbrook, Illinois.

> *"I loved ASU. I loved the weather, the grounds and, yes, even the girls. I also enjoyed my major – business – until we came to the accounting part with all the mathematics. It's as though I hit a wall. You see, unlike my dad, and even Lance, I never really understood math. My brain's simply not wired for it."*

> *"To this day, I dislike algebraic equations and geometry. Unfortunately, my job involves a lot of numbers so I hire the best accountants to crunch them for me. They know what I need to hear. I tell them, 'Hey, don't complicate this for me. You can keep your diagrams and charts. Show me the bottom line: the money. What is this going to cost us? How much are we going to make? Simple.'"* – B.J.

B.J. changed his major to communication.

A Hectic Night

"Hey, haven't you heard about the huge frat party? C'mon, we gotta go," announced B.J.'s other roommate, Tim, a.k.a. Mr. Clean. "No, man," B.J. protested. "I have a 6:00 a.m. Gotta study for it."

Our Journey: By B.J. Bohne

B.J. was already on academic probation. He didn't want to blow it. He really had to begin toning the partying down to keep his grades up. But his roommate would not relent. "Oh c'mon, it's just a couple of drinks. We'll be back in no time." Back then, there was a statewide last-call of 12:30 a.m., so he figured they'd probably be back by 1:00 a.m. at the latest.

Reluctantly, he agreed; if Clean endorsed a party, you know it was the place to be; he knew about all the hottest goings on throughout the school's entire social structure. Clean was the man!

As the night grew and the drinking ensued, the boys were soon hammered drunk. Instead of returning to their rooms, they decided to amp it up; they wanted more. Jumping into B.J.'s convertible corvette, they went in search of another party.

"It was another beautiful Arizona night – stars out, eighty-five degrees. As I came up to a stop sign, I made a left turn and gunned it. The car made a 360-degree spin."

"Well, I figured I'm in control; this is fun, so why not make a few more spins? I spun a couple more times, coming to a screeching halt right in front of a squad

Imperial Crane

A chase ensued.

As B.J. tried to negotiate a turn, they hit a bump; the car was now airborne. Crashing into two parked cars, they landed on the sidewalk and were, by then, each bleeding from minor cuts.

"Put on your seat belt, Clean!" B.J. shouted, sternly. Off they sped again right down the sidewalk, with several police cars in hot pursuit.

About five miles out, B.J. glanced in his rear-view mirror and, to his pleasant surprise, he'd actually lost the cops. With some measured relief, he figured they should try and get back to the house. By then it was almost 2:00 a.m. and the streets were practically deserted.

Pulling up to a stop sign, they realized they were right behind a Tempe, Arizona squad car. B.J. tried to remain calm, hoping the policeman wouldn't see the smoking car behind him. When he noticed the cop looking at him in his rear view mirror, he thought, "One of my lights must be out." With the top down, though, he was sure the cop could see their bloodied faces. Off in the distance, they could hear the sirens from the other cars trying to catch them.

Our Journey: By B.J. Bohne

When the light turned green, the police officer slowly inched into the intersection, allowing the other cop cars to catch up. B.J. knew he had to make a move; he cranked the steering wheel sharply to the left, gunned the gas and another chase began.

Soon, there were about seven squad cars with screaming sirens and flashing lights, all hard on the tail of B.J.'s corvette as it hit speeds over 110 m.p.h. down one of Tempe's main boulevards.

Clean totally panicked. Desperate, he tried to throw the car into neutral, as he yelled, "Stop! You're gonna kill us!"

"Relax buddy, we're gonna be fine," B.J. tried to reassure him, right before - BOOM! – part of the fiberglass body cut into the front tire and blew it out. B.J. lost control of the car and hit a street pole in the middle of the intersection, slicing the car in half.

The corvette's on fire!

"Run, Clean, run!" B.J. shouted as they climbed out of the burning car.

Clean cursed him out and started yelling to the cops, "It was him! Arrest him!" B.J. was perplexed and thinking,

Imperial Crane

"What? Me? You're the reason I'm out here in the first place. I wanted to study tonight!"

Blood splattered over his face and body, B.J. took off running.

> "Though still somewhat tipsy, I was a nineteen-year-old in tip-top physical shape completely pumped with adrenaline. I was not going to let them catch me. I jumped over backyard fences, hid in sheds, ran from dogs, and, just before dawn, came up to this really high six-foot wall with chicken wire fencing along the top. I somehow maneuvered it and landed right in the bushes of someone's yard on the other side. I was sore all over. Tired and exhausted, I collapsed in what I clearly thought to be a perfect hiding spot. I felt safe from the manhunt, which had now engaged helicopters and police dogs." – B.J.

Hours later, B.J. woke up and made his way back to Lance's condo. "Dude, what happened to you?" Lance asked. "We gotta call the old man right now!" B.J. called his father, expecting a long lecture and stern reprimand. He was totally panicked.

When John picked up the phone, B.J. began pleading for an immediate exit out of Arizona. John replied, "Listen, calm down. Calm down right now son! This is exactly what I want

Our Journey: By B.J. Bohne

you to do." John was being firm, yet very calm and reassuring. B.J. was asking himself if Dad had a plan for this; who ever had a plan for something like this? "Have your brother drive you to the nearest hospital in Mesa," he continued.

"Do not go into Tempe where you just goofed up because I don't want those guys messing with you. When you get to the hospital, have them check you out, treat you, but when they ask you what happened, tell them you don't remember. You just woke up like this, and no matter what they say, you remember nothing. Okay?'"

"But Dad, I remember everything," B.J. pleaded. "What if they ask more questions?" John sternly repeated his instructions and said he would get back in touch with his son after deliberating with his attorney.

> *"When I got back to the house that morning, it was surrounded by Tempe Police. They immediately pounced on me, thinking I was B.J." – Jeff Bohne*

Lance took him to the emergency room.

When asked what happened, he followed his dad's instructions, "I don't know. I don't remember." "Well, we gotta get you checked out and stop that bleeding," the nurse said. The doctors dutifully treated him, did an MRI and got him stabilized.

Imperial Crane

When he woke up a couple of hours later, he was hand-cuffed to the bed, with a Mesa police officer right by his side. The officer, giggling, asked, "What the heck did you do last night?"

"Sir, I don't remember," B.J. responded shyly.

"Cut it out son! I was listening on my scanner last night. You better be glad those guys didn't catch up with you. They'd have shot you!"

Then the officer said, "Look, I can wait four hours for you to get discharged and process your transfer back to Tempe; but I'm just gonna have you sign all these tickets and release you on your own recognizance. You can deal with this down the road."

The nightmare was over. B.J.'s amnesia had worked. He did do some community service but, all in all, disaster was averted.

"I remember this story as if it were yesterday because it's one of the most vivid displays of my dad's sense of composure and situational ingenuity. I don't know anyone who is always ready with an answer to any scenario, like my dad was. No matter what I needed fixed, he was always there; call him Mr. Solution. He always gave me an answer that I could take to the

Our Journey: By B.J. Bohne

*bank. It's one of the things I miss most about him." –
B.J.*

Back Home

*"As soon as I completed my communications degree, I
put my dog, Yukon, in the car along with my one duffle bag
and drove twenty-five hours straight back to Chicago; I
didn't even wait for graduation. If you
asked me what I really learned at ASU,
I'd say, "Nothing." Yeah, I've maintained that I learned absolutely nothing from all that bookwork, but maybe
that's not entirely true. As I think about
it now, the one thing college taught
me was life. Being two thousand miles
away from Mom, Dad, and my comfort zone, I learned about independence. I learned how to pay an electric
bill, a cable bill, sign a lease, live within
a budget, manage conflicts, and
maintain balance – I learned about
life; I learned about real life away from the imposing shadow
of my father's influence and protection. Those lessons would
prove invaluable to the success of my journey." – B.J.*

Travel Tip:

**Always Keep
A Cool Head.
Panicking Is
Counter-
productive!**

Three days after he returned back to Chicago, B.J. realized he was done with living at home; it didn't feel the same
anymore. So he and Yukon moved into the loft above the

80

Imperial Crane

office at Imperial Crane headquarters. It would be his home for nine years.

> *"I loved it there. I transformed one of the rooms into a gym and really made it home for me. Early in the morning, I'd listen to the crane's engines turning over, warming up before heading out for the day. I still remember the smell of the diesel fumes wafting through the vents; I shudder to think what my lungs might look like because of it." – B.J.*

John and Yukon had a love/hate relationship; maybe more hate than love. Every morning, Yukon would go down to John's office and do his morning business right there under John's desk.

Yukon literally chewed up John's beautiful leather couch and caused tens of thousands of dollars in other damages around the office.

A Beloved Mentor

> *"I chose to focus on the goal, which was to excel at the business at hand – renting and selling cranes. I discovered I was good with people and could get them to trust me. As I looked around, I saw a clear path to success doing this and knew I could add real value to Imperial Crane and to many, many others." – B.J.*

Our Journey: By B.J. Bohne

As Imperial Crane soared to become the largest crane company in Chicago, John started to loosen his grip on the day-to-day operations and pretty much left the running of the company to his childhood friend and right hand man, Jim Schmitz. Jim had friends and was well connected, which helped expose Imperial Crane to different markets around the country.

• • •

Travel Tip:

Enlist the Help Of Someone Ahead Of You To Show You the Ropes

• • •

Jim Schmitz took a keen interest in the new apprentice and decided to take him under his wing.

"So here I was at twenty-one years of age with my college degree, ready to dig in. Yes, I could operate a crane, but I really didn't know how the business worked. Thankfully, Jim took an interest in me. Living on the office premises, I was practically enslaved to Imperial Crane. At the end of the day when everyone else was gone, I was still answering calls and dealing with customers. I ran around all day with Jim from job to job, not even stopping to eat. I remember protesting one day, 'Jim, I'm hungry. I don't care what you say, but we are pulling in here and we are going to grab a sandwich.' He stopped, and from that day on, I had him hooked on Subway sandwiches." – B.J.

Imperial Crane

Although B.J. knew how to clean, operate, paint, repair, and work a crane, he knew nothing about management. So Jim taught him how to price jobs, estimate, engineer crane lifts, do accounts payable and receivable, and to perform the various other general ins-and-outs of the business. He mentored him with absolute confidence.

B.J. was his protégé, his golden boy, and he made no bones about it. He often told John, "You want someone to mind this operation–its B.J. Look no further." It is as if Jim could see in B.J. what no one else, even B.J. himself, saw. Whether he knew it or not, Jim Schmitz was grooming B.J. to take over Imperial Crane.

Jim Schmitz was one of John's most loyal friends and companions, literally to the very end; while on a phone call to John one afternoon, Jim had a stroke that tragically ended his life.

> *"Jim was running a building project for my dad while Dad was in Scotland. They were speaking on the phone, Jim sitting behind his desk in his office, when suddenly the phone died; Dad figured it was merely a problem with the phone lines. Later, when Jim missed an important business meeting with clients, they became concerned and went to check up on him; they immediately called me."*

Our Journey: By B.J. Bohne

*"I was at Citgo Refinery running another job and im-
mediately jumped into my truck and raced to the
building site to find my mentor dead on the floor." –
B.J.*

Struggles

With B.J. out of the house, and John immersed in the business and practically absent, Gayle started struggling to
breathe through their fetid marriage. Life wasn't pretty back
in the Bohne home.

*"After college, I bungeed for a while in Arizona, but
ended up back home. Going home wasn't easy;
once again, I had lost all my friends and felt somewhat alone. It was depressing. Although the crane
business was open for me because of all the opportunities, I still felt lost. I didn't really feel drawn to ventur-
ing out or trying a bunch of things. I was in my early
twenties and felt I wanted to get married and have
kids. I knew I had to settle down." – Lance*

*"Lance and I became close during the wintertime,
when Jonathan had to go back to school in Arizona.
In a way, I became close friends with both of them.
We have many interesting stories. I remember doing
180's on rainy Chicago days in deserted parking lots,*

Imperial Crane

four-wheeling out in the country, and going out to championship basketball games."

"Lance was an awesome friend, very loyal and dependable. If he couldn't get a free ticket for me to a game, he bought it. I even ended up serving in his wedding party." – Fred Hunssinger

Maybe Lance needed more from his dad than B.J. did.

• • •

Travel Tip:

**Be Very Slow To Judge.
No Matter How Much You Know, It's Not the Whole Story**

• • •

Asked by Pat whether he'd rather have his dad or the business, Lance replied, "You know what? My dad – any day. Sure, I have really struggled a lot, but I am so glad I've had my family by my side through all this. I am very grateful for my family."

"When Lance was engaged and focused, he was as good as anyone. Without a doubt, he made a truly significant contribution to the success of Imperial Crane. Do I blame Dad for our issues? I really can't. I don't think I could ever point a finger at him. Are there decisions I don't understand or maybe I could have made differently? Sure, but I am no better than him based on performance or any external factors. Because I am me, and he was his own man, I really

Our Journey: By B.J. Bohne

could not, and will never, judge him. None of us can."
– B.J.

As John's passion for golf increased, he started to spend more time at his winter home in Arizona. Gayle loved the weather and so she decided to move there, taking her last-born son with her.

> *"My mom is the person I love the most. She is amazing. I think she has been through enough, so I hesitate to even tell the ghastly details of my sad story. The last thing I want is to hurt her any more than I already have. I thank God for Mom. See, she did not grow up privileged. She knew how to work, to toil and to earn a living."*

> *"Ever since I can recall, she has emphasized modesty. 'You are blessed, but that doesn't mean you're better than anyone else.' She would say, 'Always remember: not everyone has it this well. You need to be appreciative of your life and its privileges.' So she took me to homeless shelters; we did volunteer work, and got engaged in toy drives. This helped me to not become arrogant and cocky, or to think people owed me something." – Jonathan*

As we sat down in the beautiful, lush gardens at the renowned Passages Addiction Treatment Center in Malibu,

Imperial Crane

overlooking the picturesque Pacific Ocean, Jonathan continued:

"It was after I turned six that I think it became pretty clear to my mom that she didn't really have the best husband. In trying to escape the pain and to protect me, she moved us to Arizona. As soothing as that was for her, the move separated me from my big brothers and really broke up the family. My brothers lived with my dad, over two thousand miles away. I resented it because all my friends were in Chicago. I loved coming back to Chicago."

"For at least one week every month, Dad would come to see us. He constantly hugged me, affirmed me, and told me how much he loved me. With that said, he was a very intimidating man. Everyone knew the mantra: "Whatever he says, goes." I think he knew he didn't need to be hard on me. See, whatever he said, I did; I didn't want to defy my father in any way."

"Though Dad had been fairly absent from our childhood, he was always there for Jonathan. He never missed any of his games. He constantly told him how much he loved him.

"So I asked him one day, 'Dad, how come you were different with us?' 'Well, you were born during times of

Our Journey: By B.J. Bohne

struggle. Not him. I am going to try something different with him. He is never going to have to work a day in his life' replied Dad. 'Well,' I said, 'Let me know how that goes.'" – B.J.

And sure enough, life did indeed become a challenge for the young, over-gratified and enormously privileged Jonathan Bohne.

"In my opinion, Jonathan had a tremendous upbring-ing. I mean, a mom like Gayle; who wouldn't want to have a mom like that? She is a dream! But I think by the time he got to high school, he had done every-thing there was to do. He'd been on great trips and vacations; he'd been there, done that. With his re-sources at that age, he could get into anything he wanted to. I remember him coming back from school one day and introducing us to some new drug."

"While it was cool at the time, the story started to change as we all grew older. It wasn't funny anymore. I remember pleading with him to slow down on many a dark night. I would go out with him just so there was someone with him to stop him from falling off the edge. I felt as though I was condoning bad behavior, but I believed it was better that he had someone with him to at least make sure he got home at night." – Fred Hunssinger

Imperial Crane

"I remember the first time I was arrested. I was in seventh grade and started using, and had brought pot to school. I was also into alcohol, so I had my brothers get some for my friends and I. One day, Lance said, 'I want you to go get something for me at this address,' and handed me a set of directions. We were thrilled. See, at fifteen years old, we were looking forward to driving a car, inexperienced as we were. 'Now when you get stopped by the police, just say you took the car without my permission, okay?' So we pulled up into some neighborhood in the ghetto. Everyone ran up to the car, surprised to see three kids in Lance's car. 'We want four twenties for sixty,' we nervously demanded, as Lance had instructed us. We got our stash and sped away. We had just bought crack cocaine."
– Jonathan

After years of struggling with addiction, at the time of this writing, Jonathan has taken a courageous step in the right direction: sobriety. He is working on a complete life-change. I was truly privileged to enjoy a most engaging conversation with him, and as we ended our interview, he looked squarely in my eyes and said, "Dr. Dennis, I am the kid who lost his virginity at twelve; who started smoking before I was even a teenager. I have been held up at gunpoint, pistol whipped, overdosed, had three stints in county jail, two DUIs in two states, had countless arrests in three states, hired prostitutes, meddled with strippers, loved crazy girlfriends,

Our Journey: By B.J. Bohne

and suffered a mountain of bad things. Here I am a millionaire, hanging out in crack houses in Cabrini Green.

At twenty-nine, I have too many war stories for my age. I don't want this anymore. Ironically, I had to have these grotesque things happen to me so I could wake up. I know there are a million people who would kill to have the opportunities I have had. I have been so blessed; I regret all the wasted years. I don't want to have to use a substance to get out of bed or just to feel normal. I realize that right now, I have a big decision to make: to either keep walking this direction, which might mean death in a few years, or to take a completely new path where I become a respectable member of society, eventually get married to a good girl, and have beautiful babies. Heck, I don't even think I've ever had a sober date; I've literally been high on something on all the dates I can remember. So, I am looking forward to a new life ahead for me."

Travel Tip:

As Long As You Have Breath, It Is Never Too Late To Turn Your Ship Around

"Would I give John a "Father-of-the-Year trophy"? Probably not, but he sure did all he could to provide for his boys." – Jeff Bohne

90

Imperial Crane

I was so honored to spend a couple days with Jim Bohne in his beautiful summer home in magnificent Minocqua, Wisconsin. We talked for hours as he shared countless experiences of the family history and his own long journey. As my visit ended, my teary-eyed, tired host made this sobering statement, "As their uncle, I spent many days regretting my lack of involvement in their lives. I often wish I had done more for the boys. Maybe I could have taken them under my wing and mentored them. Maybe, somehow, I could have helped them avoid some of those pitfalls and prevented some of the pain they've suffered. But I also know there are choices I could not have prevented. At the end of the day, each one of us has to take ownership of our own decisions. When I think about that, I find some relief. I know there are some things you cannot prevent, even with the best advice."

Chapter Travel Tips

#8: Do Not Put Kids In The Middle of A Grownup Fight

Relationship tension is common to all of us. It gets especially complicated when children are involved. As tempting as it may be to try and get kids to pick sides, parents must refrain. It is irresponsible to put emotionally immature children in the middle of adult squabbles. It only confuses them, and scars them. Often for life.

#9: Always Keep A Cool Head. Panicking Is Counter-productive

When faced with unexpected situations, there are two ways to respond: panic and blow up, or breathe and calmly maneuver. Panicking constricts your ability to reason and stifles creativity. It floods your emotions and makes you susceptible to impulsivity. Prayer is a great way to help you breathe. The Psalmist wrote, "Cast your cares on the LORD and he will sustain you." (Psalms 55:22 NIV)

#10: Enlist The Help Of Someone Ahead Of You To Show You The Ropes

You might call them influencers, teachers, instructors, or coaches. Like Jim Schmitz, they see untapped potential within you. They are convinced that you can become more than what you are. No matter who you are, you will reach a point on your journey where you could use a helping hand.

Our Journey: By B.J. Bohne

There are certain decisions that have potential to greatly and permanently impact your life. It might be a marriage decision, a career change or a resolution to start a family. In such cases, you will need someone to help you muddle through the different options and emotions, and show you the ropes. Remember, their job is not to celebrate your achievements, they are there to help you unleash your potential; they are more concerned about your future and what you can become.

#11: Be Very Slow To Judge. No Matter How Much You Know, It's Not The Whole Story

We live in a culture that is extremely judgmental. Everyone seems to have an opinion about everyone else's circumstances. Having grown up in the church, and being in ministry, I was often quick to point fingers at the heathen, sinners or those who weren't walking the straight and narrow. After traveling to over sixty-three countries and sitting with people from all walks of life, I think differently now; I'm not so quick to judge anymore. Before you put your finger in someone else's face, ask this: If I had the same circumstances, the same fears, the same environment and personality, how different from them would I really be?

#12: As Long As You Have Breath, It Is Never Too Late To Turn Your Ship Around

Whether it is Beethoven, Einstein, Thomas Edison, Walt Disney, or Abraham Lincoln, all truly successful people learn how to embrace adversity, setbacks, and failure as part of their journey. It is said that only 10 percent of life is made up of what happens to you—the other 90 percent is how you respond to what happens to you. Granted that today is a result of yesterday's decisions, God has given you the power

Imperial Crane

to choose the direction your life should take. It does not matter what yesterday has brought into your life. The question is: what are you going to write on the clean slate of your tomorrow? May you be comforted with these words, "For I know the plans I have for you," says the Lord. 'They are plans for good and not for disaster, to give you a future and a hope.'" (Jeremiah 29:11 NLT)

When You Clean Up a Weed Patch

When you clean up a weed patch
It will never stay bare.
When you plant a little garden
You must tend it with care.

There's a good time to sow;
Next comes labor, sun, and rain.
Now comes the ripe time for harvest
And you can hope for a gain.

The sower and reaper work very hard –
Some years will be good and some will be bad.
It takes planning, work, and courage
To harvest the best, young lad – so like your dad.

Willadene
"A Child Can Dream and other Poems and Prose"
Copyright 1981

"For I know the plans I have for you", says the LORD. 'They are plans for good and not for disaster, to give you a future and a hope.'"

Jeremiah 29:11 (NLT)

-W. Nicholas

Part Two: The Company

Chapter 4

John's Company

"From the minute I met him, I knew that someday John would be very successful. The man always talked about his dreams."

– Gayle Bohne

"Why don't you buy my apartment buildings?"

"What? How do you think I could possibly afford that?"

"Well, let me take you to my bank. We will sit down with the president and get you financed. See, I am retiring soon and, yeah, I like you, kid."

Thus went a conversation between John and his landlord that would change the trajectory of John's life.

A Game Changer

A couple of days later, he was sitting in the bank president's office, signing a loan for his first apartment building.

Our Journey: By B.J. Bohne

As soon as he bought the units, he rented them out and started to make some money. But instead of spending the profits or even saving the cash, he dumped it all into another purchase, acquiring his second apartment building; eventually, John would own five apartment buildings. It was during this time that he met his long-time friend, Larry Gedmin, a.k.a. Whitey. At the time of this writing, forty-six years later, Larry is still associated with the family and currently runs Imperial Crane's Indiana offices.

John was selling insurance during the day, and operating cranes for Canon Steel Erectors at night; all this while also managing his apartment buildings. An apartment owner's greatest woe is delinquent tenants, but John was a no-nonsense landlord; when a tenant fell back on their rent, he would get a moving truck, nicely box up all their belongings and move them to a storage unit. That little exercise proved very effective, notwithstanding the legal implications that would render it impractical today. When the panicked renters walked into an empty apartment, they seemed eager to find the money.

Years later, he would follow the same principle with his cranes. His mantra was: "You never mess with the asset." One day, he learned his cranes were being damaged by debris at a work site. He immediately drove out to persuade the renter to better protect his equipment. When the renter talked back to him, basically telling him to suck it up and

Imperial Crane

shut up, John unhesitatingly demanded that his operators immediately pack up and get ready to roll out. The bewildered renter had an immediate change of mind.

Yes, he believed in favors, and in being in the right place at the right time, but John also knew there was more to success than luck; real success requires diligence and responsibility.

Our First Crane

While there are varying, even incongruent, accounts of exactly how this great company started, I have elected to render B.J.'s version, as told to him directly by his father.

During the spring of 1969, John and Whitey worked for a small crane company known as Cannon Steel Erection. They got hired to do a crane job by Bill Boehm for his company, Imperial Components, and were to set roof trusses for a massive apartment building project.

When they learned the job would take two years to complete, Cannon Steel Erection became uneasy. The last thing

Our Journey: By B.J. Bohne

Jack McKabe, Cannon's supervisor, wanted to do was tie up a crane for that long. Crane businesses have always been more interested in the lucrative daily rental business than in less profitable, long-term projects. "If this job is going to take two years, then we're out of here," McKabe protested.

That got John's attention, so he proposed, "If these guys really want to rent a crane for two years, why don't I buy one and rent it to them?" Reluctantly, Jack agreed.

John approached Bill Boehm with his idea, and the two formed a partnership. They would buy a crane – their own crane – and rent it out to Imperial Components. But there was a problem: they could not afford it; they didn't have that kind of cash.

John decided to go visit his favorite bank president – the same guy who had financed his apartment buildings. His plan was to use his apartment buildings to collateralize a loan for his first crane. This was insanely risky.

The apartments were providing much needed supplemental cash flow. It was great to have that certain influx of revenue from the investment for his family. Eliminating it for something that was yet uncertain was a huge gamble.

The loan got approved and the two purchased their first crane shortly thereafter.

Imperial Crane

"I was involved with John initially, but I didn't have the stomach to build a business on credit. I wasn't too sure about waiting years to get my money out. I was more like my dad. For most of those early years, John ran everything on a shoestring budget. When you look at our family background, we are farmers. We plant, we wait, and then we reap. Basically, you don't eat what you haven't grown. When I think back to my forty aunties and uncles, I don't remember any of them ever buying cars on credit. They didn't have credit cards, or even carry mortgages. My dad built his house and paid for everything by cash. It is how he raised us. Actually, none of us were like John. He was a risk taker, and we all respected him for it. In the long run, I think his way is better."

Travel Tip:

Be Prepared To Leverage Your Gains For Greater Opportunities

"Today, I certainly could use the steady revenue that Imperial Crane enjoys. Although he didn't go to college, he was smart enough to read the trends; to know that credit was the way of the future. In many ways, it's as though John had a crystal ball. I still remember years later when we first saw a five hundred ton crane. Nobody I knew in the industry would even dare buy such a large crane. Well, John did, and be-

Our Journey: By B.J. Bohne

fore long, only Imperial Crane could service a certain caliber of jobs. He was always way ahead of the game." – Jim Bohne

Imperial Crane

John and Bill Boehm decided to go with the name Imperial Crane. "When they went out to work with Bill Boehm's company," recalls B.J. "Dad was taken by the name, Imperial. He liked the sound of it, and what it stood for."

As soon as the crane arrived at the site, they promptly painted the word **IMPERIAL** on it. They did this so potential clients would assume an association with an established company, Imperial Components. The name also provided the benefit of warding off other crane companies that would try to come in and cut their rates.

With John still working at Cannon Steel Erection, along with his insurance day job, and Bill Boehm rather busy with Imperial Components, they had to hire someone to run the crane. Thus, they hired operators from the local union. This practice, though, seemed to breed constant headaches.

What they needed was a full-time operator, but much as they tried, no one seemed to be willing to commit to the job. John had even tried to persuade his cousin Fred Bohne, but

Imperial Crane

he also declined. To most, the venture seemed much too risky.

Finally, John made Whitey an offer, "Hey, we can't keep going like this. The union is driving me nuts! I need a full-time operator for our crane; someone stable and reliable. Will you come run the crane for me? Tell you what; I'll even get you into the union."

Whitey agreed, and left his job to work full-time with John. At the same time, John decided it was time to quit his insurance job and throw everything into the crane business. While the local unions and almost everyone else they knew were skeptical about the prospects of this risky undertaking, John never showed any signs of doubt.

With the first crane committed to the Imperial Components project, John went out and purchased a second crane. Gayle remembers the day he told her. "I freaked out. How were we going to afford this? As it was, the monthly note alone seemed impossible."

John told her they'd be fine, "Gayle, just take the calls. And no matter where the job is, tell them 'Yes, we will do it', and we'll be there. I'll figure out a way to make it all work."

He spent the next few months soliciting new business from anyone who would listen, be they rail companies, schools or

Our Journey: By B.J. Bohne

other large corporations. As the momentum built, he purchased a third crane. With that, Imperial Crane could now set air conditioners, do steel projects and schools all at the same time.

Business was booming, and the company now needed an office – a real office. He approached an old friend, Sid Duncan, and proposed a merger: the two would share business premises in Oak Lawn, Illinois.

Imperial Crane now had someone to answer the phones and take orders, but they urgently needed storage space for the cranes.

> *"We started renting garages, but that didn't work out, especially in the winter when the frigid Chicago temperatures hit. We would light up a canister of oil to warm the cranes."*

> *"Today, we would be put in jail for doing that – it's too dangerous. I remember renting this one garage that had a really mean dog; that dog terrorized me to no end. Fed up, I threatened to quit, so we moved again." – Larry (Whitey) Gedmin*

Eventually, they found some rental space from Bob Kucher, an excellent engineer, whom John eventually brought aboard to join them.

Imperial Crane

"Dad was great at leveraging. He leveraged an apartment building to buy a second one, then three to buy five. Then he leveraged all that to buy his first crane, then two, until he built a massive company. That, to me, was his genius." – B.J.

Imperial Crane continued to grow. They purchased their first thirty ton hydraulic truck crane, and in 1972 erected their first office building in Palos, Illinois.

A Critical Partnership

"Hey, you want to buy Bill Boehm out for $5000?" asked John.

"Are you crazy," Whitey replied, "why would I do that? All this seems good for now, but man, I'm not so sure about the long-term prospects here. Besides, I have no money."

John would return to Whitey with the same proposition as the business grew: Seventy-five hundred; then ten thousand; Whitey would not bite. He did not have the confidence to take the leap; a decision he regrets to this day.

When Bill Boehm encountered some family difficulties, he became disinterested in the business and wanted to be bought out.

Our Journey: By B.J. Bohne

Whitey's brother, Jimmy Gedmin, was playing softball and Whitey invited John to one of the games. Cloyd Selby and Ron Selby Sr. were also there. As the game ensued, John and Cloyd, who had previously worked together on some jobs, got to talking. By the end of the night, the two had decided to join forces. With Cloyd's engineering brain and John's financing wizardry, John knew they could take *Imperial Crane* to the next level. John offered him the opportunity to buy Bill Bohme out for $25,000. Cloyd took the deal and a new partnership was born.

Cloyd brought his group on board, which meant that now Imperial Crane had a team of office staff. Most importantly, Cloyd had collateral, which was gold to John. He immediately took the equity out of Cloyd's house and leveraged it to purchase a new eighty-two ton Link Belt crane.

The duo would embark on their first high profile job: The Oakbrook Hyatt in Chicago. The project would give Imperial Crane great visibility and attracted more business, as the company's capacity grew even further.

> *"John was always big on perceptions. He didn't want anyone thinking he ran a small company, so he painted all his cranes with different colors. Some were red, green, blue, yellow – all designed to create the impression that he was a large company. And you know what? It worked!" – Jim Bohne*

Imperial Crane

"I came on board right after my brother Cloyd teamed up with John. With his mechanical expertise and John's business brain, it was a wonderful partnership. My brother could keep the cranes running while John kept the business coming. John let each of us pick our favorite color to paint our cranes, so it looked as though we had a bunch of them. Everyone was talking about the company with all the different colored cranes. We only had a handful, but it looked like we had more than a hundred." - Ron Selby Sr.

● ● ●

Travel Tip:

As You Embark On Your Success Journey, You Must Find Your Travel Mates

"When I asked him why all the colors," recalls B.J., "Dad told me he thought he had seen the idea work well for an airline company. When he saw something that worked, he ran with it. Dad recognized great concepts and was not bashful to replicate them if he could."

● ● ●

"John's thinking was that although we were not big yet, we soon would be; so we had to act big! We started transitioning from hydraulic cranes to the much bigger friction cranes. In fact, we ended up buying a two hundred ton friction crane; the biggest in the Midwest. That was pretty radical in those days. They

Our Journey: By B.J. Bohne

wanted to build a fast and efficient operation; if we could do two jobs while everyone else did only one, we could get by with half the number of cranes." - Ron Selby Sr.

For the next few months, John was busy making bigger deals, connecting with clients and building camaraderie with his growing team. It was not uncommon to find him hanging out in one of his operator's backyards on a Sunday afternoon enjoying a barbeque and a live Mariachi band.

"I Want To Hire Bill"

Bill Tierney worked for a major full-line equipment distribu-tor. It was a very secure desk job with full benefits in what was then a struggling construction industry. He had recently been promoted to Link Belt product manager and was, frankly, happy where he was.

He had previously rented cranes from John and Cloyd, who now owned seven cranes; a really big deal at the time.

"I want to hire Bill. We need him. He would be good for us," said John to Cloyd.

"You're right. He is great, John, but there is no way we will ever get him. He is happy where he is; just got promoted,

Imperial Crane

with a good package in a safe company." "Doesn't matter to me," quipped John, "Let's make him an offer."'

John called Bill Tierney who predictably declined their offer, and replied, "My boss has been good to me and I don't want to mess up anything here. Even if I wanted to go, how do I get out of this?"

That got John even more interested; he loved challenges! So he said to Bill, "Well, let me handle getting you out of that; that's my specialty."

A few days later, Bill was called into his boss's office.

"You know John wants you," Bill's boss said. Bill Tierney was embarrassed and went into a long apologetic rant about his loyalty, but was interrupted.

"Well, I want you to know that although we would never want to lose you, I also don't want to hinder you. If John wants you as badly as he says, then there might be something there for you to consider. Feel free to talk to him."

"To this day, I don't know how John pulled that off or what he told my boss, but a couple of days later, he and I met and he made me an offer I simply couldn't refuse. At the time, the crane industry was just beginning to develop. Not many people had multiple

117

Our Journey: By B.J. Bohne

cranes, so I was excited to be part of his vision. Clearly, John was on to something." – Bill Tierney

Bill Tierney joined the management team at Imperial Crane in 1978. He oversaw operations and managed home base while John and the team were out executing on the contracts and expanding the business.

"John spent a lot of time courting customers and chasing new business. The minute he saw an opportunity, he was all over it. He never procrastinated. But he needed Bill to run the daily operations of the company. I think the best thing John did for Imperial Crane was to hire Bill." – Sam Palumbo, John's long-time friend

"John was constantly buying more cranes, borrowing more money, and growing the business. To everyone else in the crane business, it was the wrong time to expand. As crane manufacturers slashed prices, he bought as many cranes as he could find banks to loan him the money. I would say to him, 'John, this is insane. Let's pace ourselves. Interest rates are not great. Let's slow down some.' He would respond, 'Bill, I told you that I don't care how we gotta do it, but if a crane becomes available, we are buying it.' Clearly, I was the conservative one who constantly pulled back. John was the visionary. All he saw was more growth,

Imperial Crane

more expansion, bigger opportunities and greater risks. In hindsight, it was great for the company and our relationship that we did not always see eye to eye on many issues. And although we fought about many directional decisions, he knew he needed my opinion." – Bill Tierney

As the explosive growth continued, Bill Tierney recognized they needed someone to help manage the manpower. He tapped his brother John, who at the time worked for Chicago Northwestern Railroad, to join the company. John Tierney would later become one of Imperial Crane's most valuable employees and remains so to this day.

I had the privilege of spending a few minutes with John Tierney. His refreshing attitude about life and his rich thirty-three year history with the company is nothing short of remarkable. You couldn't find a happier employee.

"I am so grateful Bill introduced me to John. At first, I thought he was arrogant. Most everybody did, but that's not it; he was confident. He knew what he wanted, and was not quiet about it. I, for one, didn't have any problem with that; it meant you knew exactly what he expected of you. If you had an issue with anything, he was open to suggestions. His door was always open, although not many ventured in to question him. What made him such an awesome boss was

Our Journey: By B.J. Bohne

that when he delegated a job, he never intruded. He let you fly. He treated my brother and me better than any other employer ever would have." – John Tierney

Without a doubt, John understood people and their potential. He made relationships with people who had the strengths he needed.

A Game-Changing Job

"Hey Whitey, you gotta go see this guy. He is looking for you urgently," John announced. Whitey was resistant at first. Months before, he had done a small job for one of the largest construction companies in the nation and now Dave, the owner, was looking for him.

Whitey decided to go hear Dave out, not anticipating the weight of his proposal. He told him, "Whitey, I liked your performance on that last job. I've got another deal for you. Will you guys run a major construction project for me? I will need you to run the dump trucks, pickup trucks, the welding machines, everything. Think you can handle it?"

Whitey emphatically agreed, even though he wasn't yet able to wrap his head around the enormous task. He ran the offer by John, who really encouraged him to take it, despite the fact it was undoubtedly over Whitey's head. Whitey

Imperial Crane

wanted to back out, even though it was a $50 million project.

When he returned the following day, he learned he had misheard the value of the job; it was actually a mind-boggling $500 million venture. In 1977, that was a truckload of money. He struggled to collect himself, and promptly accepted the job.

> *"That one job turned Imperial Crane into a multi-million dollar crane company. We grew to over eighty employees, and for the next three years, we rolled in the big bucks. Almost every week, I would walk away with a $400 thousand check for Imperial Crane. That was way more money than we had ever seen. What was interesting was John didn't even show up at the site but maybe three times. He had complete trust in me."*
> *– Whitey*

Even with the success, John never took anything for granted. He was fanatical about timekeeping. The staff, operators and teams absolutely had to keep correct time; he paid the guys well, and figured they owed him that much. One thing they all knew was that if they worked hard, he would take care of them, no matter what.

> *"He put his life into this company. I remember him calling at least three times a day no matter where he was.*

Our Journey: By B.J. Bohne

Unlike most bosses, he could do any of our jobs. If something happened to an operator at a site, say they fell ill or something, it was not uncommon to see John drive to the job in his Cadillac, jump into the crane dressed in his suit, make the lift, fold the crane up, get back in his caddy and get home. If he wanted something done, he did it. He was always worried about the health of the company and the well-being of his boys." – John Tierney

Alliances

Cloyd Selby introduced many of his family members to Imperial Crane.

"It was my uncle Cloyd who introduced me to Imperial Crane. I started at the bottom as a shop kid, washing cars and cranes, servicing vehicles, cleaning floors, you name it. I remember working as John's driver for a number of years."

"Eventually, I got my operator's permit with the union. I tried to look for another job after I graduated from college, but the money just didn't compare. What I made operating cranes during the summer was more than what the accounting field afforded me all year. So I stayed and kept working with John and my uncle." – Ron Selby Jr.

Imperial Crane

"I owe a lot of what I know to Ron Selby Sr.; he was one of my mentors, and one tough guy. He was your old-school crane operator who thoroughly knew his craft, in and out. He helped us define our ethos and distinctive ethic. With operating engineers from the local unions populating our employment rosters, it had always been a challenge to build loyalty. Ron helped us cultivate a spirit of loyalty amongst the operators toward the company." – B.J.

As the company grew and the boys got more and more involved, John knew the handwriting was on the wall. John owned 51 percent of the business, while Cloyd owned 49 percent. It was only a matter of time before their partnership would be faced with an awkward and complicated succession conundrum.

In 1986, John bought Cloyd out for a seven-figure amount to retain sole ownership of Imperial Crane.

A year later, Grove Worldwide, a crane manufacturer, approached Imperial Crane to distribute their aerial platforms in Chicago. John immediately called Cloyd, "I have a great idea, Cloyd," he said, "Why don't you run with this man-lift business for Grove and start your own company?" Cloyd agreed, and in 1989 he launched his man-lift venture, Selby's Aero Squad. His nephew, Ron Selby, followed him shortly thereafter. Cloyd did very well for himself, eventually selling that business for over $10 million.

John and Cloyd were able to enjoy an enduring friendship through the years well beyond Cloyd's tenure with Imperial Crane. Cloyd remained supportive of the company even after John passed away, often taking time to check up on B.J. "My brother wanted to help the company succeed," said Ron Selby Sr. "He was always available if they ever needed anything."

B.J. and Lance would go off to college while John, Bill Tierney and Jim Schmitz ran the business.

> *"Dad never held grudges and often kept an open-door policy with his relationships. He did the same thing with Jack McKabe, his supervisor who encouraged and supported him to buy his first crane. He remained amicable even after they went their separate ways. Years later, Jack would return to work for John. The two of them maintained a friendship 'till the day he passed away." – B.J.*

As business continued to grow, a rift began to develop between Bill Tierney and Jim Schmitz. The problem was, the two shared almost equal responsibility, but they could not stand each other.

Imperial Crane

"Jim was personal friends with John and the family; they had been childhood buddies. He was also really close to B.J., and the two did a lot together. To me, it seemed as though Jim thought their friendship trumped everything. As the antagonism grew, John knew something had to give. In our business, reputation is key; it's how people perceive your company or brand that really counts. Our bickering did not look good for the company, so John bought another business and put Jim in charge of that, effectively separating us. I think that one move was the best thing John did for the company. Now, I know that this is a big statement and some might not agree with me, but knowing what I know, I stand by it. With Jim Schmitz gone, I got the opportunity to help craft our brand the way I thought we needed to. I know how this sounds, but I have no ego issues, so I don't really care what people think of me. My commitment is to continue to build our brand, and to that end, I have given the better part of the last thirty-five years of my life." – Bill Tierney

• • •

Travel Tip:

To Enjoy Sustained Success, Be Ready To Change Alliances

• • •

John invited Ron Selby Jr. back to *Imperial Crane* to serve as part of his management team. Ron heartily agreed but asked for a favor, conditional upon the successful execution

Our Journey: By B.J. Bohne

of his new managerial duties. Ron asked for a line of credit to help him launch the man-lift business under *Imperial Crane*. John agreed and, sure enough, six months later he made good on his promise. Ron's division took off as John increased his credit line from year to year. "When John and I shook hands on something, John's word was good no matter what. B.J.'s is the same way. When you have a conversation, you know that he will keep his end of the bargain," recollects Ron.

Though he never involved B.J. in any executive decision-making, John had his eye on him. He invited him to attend closed-door meetings with banks, unions and insurance companies. They golfed together as he courted clients for business.

> *"I remember going to ask Dad for a raise one morning. 'You want to make more money? Don't ask me for it. You go make more money!' Definitely not the response I was looking for. Then he said, 'Listen, I'll be golfing in Arizona, but you guys go run with it. Use my credibility with the banks and insurance companies. I will support you however you need to be supported.'"*

> *"Clearly, he had accomplished far more than he hoped for, and I think he was beginning to settle."* – B.J.

Imperial Crane

For the next several years, they grew the business tenfold, to over $30 million in annual revenue, while also tripling their fleet of cranes. All the while, and rather interestingly, John never raised his salary at all. While he immensely enjoyed the benefits, merely making boatloads of money was not John's top aim; he wanted to be a force in the crane business in the city of Chicago and beyond. He courted city officials, power brokers, the mayor and governors. He was mindful of the real threat of outside crane companies trying to under-cut his rates and take his contracts. John kept his eye on the prize: to build people and to build Imperial Crane Services.

"I am a fourth generation crane operator. My grand-father, Richard Bohne, was John Bohne's first cousin. I always referred to him as my uncle John and to his sons as my cousins. I remember all of us growing up together. I even stood in B.J.'s wedding; we all go way back! I wouldn't be here without this company. I started, in 1996, at the very bottom, sweeping floors while attending Easter Illinois University. Later, I was moved up to crane operator. I was in my first semester at medical school when I decided to quit university. Naturally, my academic counselor encouraged me to pursue opportunities in the medical field, but when he learned how much money I made operating a crane during holidays and breaks, he suggested I go back to work. When John learned, through Lance's recom-mendation, that I was available full time, he hired me

Our Journey: By B.J. Bohne

back to manage the parts and service department and to run the shop in the main location in Bridgeview. At the time, Imperial Crane owned less than forty cranes." – Larry Eckardt, Vice President of operations at Imperial Crane services.

"As early as I can remember, John was an astute businessman. He always seemed to know exactly what he wanted, and boy did he have a nose for a good deal. I watched him fight with the unions, negotiate with insurance companies, win over high-powered clients and grow our team of employees. He mentored me, and I took it all in. I would not be nearly as successful as I am today without John Bohne." – Whitey

Chapter Travel Tips

#13: God Will Sometimes Place People In Your Life To Show You Favor. Honor Their Kindness With Diligence

Whether it is the boss who takes to you, the banker who approves your loan without sufficient collateral, or the girl you don't deserve who shockingly says "Yes," sometimes God will cause people to show you unmerited favor. That's fantastic, but favor alone isn't enough. When doors are opened for you, be ready to walk through them. Beyond that, though, you must be ready to work. There is no such thing as a handout to success. Favor must be accompanied by corresponding action, which is PLAIN HARD WORK!

#14: Be Prepared To Leverage Your Gains For Greater Opportunities

Successful people are not safe players. They take risks; sometimes very big risks. There are times when life will dare you to take all your gains and throw them in for a greater hand. Make no mistake, sometimes the gamble doesn't work. Sometimes you will throw it in and lose everything. But until you take that first step, you will never know. The journey to success is also a journey of faith. You must confidently believe in your next step, even when it may not completely make sense.

Our Journey: By B.J. Bohne

#15: As You Embark On Your Success Journey, You Must Find Your Travel Mates

No one climbs to the top alone. Success requires that we enlist people to walk with us. It is an indisputable fact that when you walk with the wrong people, you suffer losses. Conversely, when you walk with the right people, you will enjoy safety and success. John knew that very well. He knew he could not make it alone, but he also understood the principle that not everyone could play on his team.

#16: To Enjoy Sustained Success, Be Ready To Change Alliances

Sometimes, as in the hit TV show Survivor, you will need to change teams or let some people go, in order to create new alliances. In my books, I call them the now-people and the then-people. Then-people were good then. They might have been helpful and important then, but unless they continue to add value to your journey, they quickly become inconvenient, heavy and cumbersome. Their primary wish is to have the old you back. So I encourage you to take an inventory of your team, your friends and associates. Do they add to you or not? Have they outlived their effectiveness? If so, I would encourage you to consider changing your alliances; to letting them go.

I Put My Hand On Destiny

I put my hand on Destiny
Said the tyrant to the Man.
I would rule the world my way ---
But to my dismay, I have found He had a plan.

I was cruel and selfish ---
Others mattered not to me.
I paid the price soon after
I put my hand on Destiny.
Said the tyrant, "How I suffered
When my sinful ways were found.
I needed Him to rescue me
From sins that had me bound."

I put my hand on Destiny
Said the bully to the Man
All the world would cower before me ---
But to my dismay there was another plan.

I put my hand on Destiny
Said the law-breaker to the Man.
The whole world was filled with chaos
Until He revealed his plan.

I put my hand on Destiny
Said the cheater to the Man
And Trust collapsed by failures

Our Journey: By B.J. Bohne

As seen throughout the land.
I put my hand on Destiny
Said the exploiter to the Man
But it didn't really end up right
Because, you see, He had a better plan.

Willadene
"Angel Children, Rainbows of Love, Dreams are Forever and other
Poems"
Copyright 1981

"Take a lesson from the ants, you lazy-bones. Learn from their ways and be wise! Even though they have no prince, governor, or ruler to make them work, they labor hard all summer, gathering food for the winter."

Proverbs 6:6-8 (NLT)

Chapter 5

John's Playbook

"We called him 'The General' for his sharp wit, his no-nonsense approach to life and his incredible nose for the deal. When John started preaching, everyone had to just shut up and listen."

– Sam Palumbo

<u>"Come Bungee With Us For $50"</u>

That's the memo Jeff and his buddies sent out to as many friends and Arizona State University students as they could reach.

The following Saturday morning they met in a grocery store parking lot, waiting to convoy out to the nearby city of Flagstaff, Arizona with the ten respondents. With a winch military shock-cord and repelling harnesses, they would jump off the bridge. Thus was the beginning of a fad – the bungee jumping craze. As word spread, the number of participants grew and the convoys swelled to fifty cars each weekend.

Our Journey: By B.J. Bohne

"One by one, we would take their cash and throw them off bridges. They wanted more, and they kept coming for more. Soon we were raking in $5,000 a weekend. Word spread as guys and gals told their friends: 'Dude, I just did the most insane thing I've ever done. I jumped off a bridge with those crazy guys! Can't wait to go back!' I felt like a legal drug dealer. Here I was, an eighteen-year-old, making thousands of dollars a weekend." – Jeff Bohne

The police finally caught up with them and the railroad authority sued them for liability reasons. They were fined $20,000.

In their arrogance, they made a mockery of the judgment by openly paying the fine in cash, right there in court. The splash made the front-page news. This attracted the Internal Revenue Service, who immediately launched an inquiry, eventually fining them an additional $80,000, which effectively zeroed all their gains.

"When I got back to Chicago, my buddies and I started talking again. We dreamed of continuing the jumping, but we'd been burned. One of my buddies queried, 'Hey, your uncle's cranes. How high do those things really go?' This made me think. What if we could bungee jump using Uncle John's cranes? Was it even possible? We devised a plan to approach Uncle

Imperial Crane

John and make him a sound business proposition to use his cranes based on our Arizona success. It was a long-shot, perhaps, but we were definitely on to something." – Jeff Bohne

John looked at the numbers, and immediately saw the business sense in the venture; he would give them a couple of cranes; a sixty-ton and a forty-ton. First, in return for the use of the cranes, he would keep 50 percent of all the revenues. Second, they had to agree to do it right.

"When he agreed to do it, we were ecstatic. We really didn't care too much about the details. We trusted John. But none of us knew how serious he was about his last condition." – Jeff Bohne

Bungee Over Arizona

John incorporated Bungee Over Arizona, secured an amusement license and purchased insurance from Lloyds of London. He leased a large piece of property at a train yard close to Arizona State University where he put up fully furnished offices for folks to register and weigh in before they jumped. John had a goal to bring the same safety culture of Imperial Crane to the bungee jumping industry, so he made the guys use three harnesses instead of one, had the clients jumping over an Olympic-sized swimming pool, and ensured all the operators were adequately trained in an effort to

Our Journey: By B.J. Bohne

minimize any potential liability. In short, John turned an amateur past-time vocation into a professional, well-managed business venture. That was classic John Bohne.

"John never did anything half-heartedly. When he took up tennis, he got formal training. When he decided to play Gin, he went to Vegas and enrolled in Gin school. When he got into golf, he constantly took golfing lessons."

Travel Tip:

If You're Gonna Do Something, You'd Better Do It Right

"When he became curious about flying, he jumped into it with both feet, eventually buying his own planes. He wanted excellence and expected it of others in return."

– Jim Bohne

The cranes were mounted two hundred feet in the air, Gayle set up her hot-dog stand on the site, and Bungee Over Arizona was open for business.

As the clients began jumping, folks stopped in their cars in order to see the phenomenon, backing up traffic all around the vicinity. News teams from television and radio caught wind of it and word spread like wildfire. Long lines immedi-

Imperial Crane

ately formed, resulting in a first weekend take of more than $10,000.

Before they closed shop that evening, the guys wanted to split the money as they had done with their smaller operation. John said, "I understand, but here's what we're looking at." He began to lay out the total investment cost, which included the lease, ground staff, licenses, operator costs, and the upkeep. He gave them a few hundred dollars apiece; they were clearly not amused. John didn't care; this was a business, and as long as he was involved, it would be run like one.

The craze kept growing and their diligence soon paid off. Bungee Over Arizona flourished, bringing in hundreds of thousands of dollars.

> *"We would weigh them and drop them down, enough to dip their hands into the pool below, springing back up two hundred feet in the air. We had couples get married on the bungee, and even had an eighty-year-old man do a televised jump on Good Morning America." – Jeff Bohne*

The following year, John decided to bring the business to Chicago. Right there in the front yard of Imperial Crane, he dug an Olympic-sized pool and put up two sixty-ton cranes. Bungee Over Chicago was born.

Our Journey: By B.J. Bohne

Cars would line up along the freeway to see Chicagoans jump off of two cranes into a large swimming pool. No one budged even when traffic police threatened them with tickets and fines. It was spectacular. And because they had two jumpers at a time, the guys doubled their revenue.

"Who is the person in charge here?"

"That's me. How can I help you, officers?" John replied as he stepped up to talk to the two state troopers.

"Well sir, you are going to have to cease and desist here. You are creating a gridlock on the toll-way with all this jump-ing."

"Excuse me," John shot back, as he prepared to ask a few pointed questions of his own, "is this Illinois property? Are we breaking any laws?"

"No sir," replied the cop.

"Well then, I don't for the life of me see how this is any of our problem. I would suggest you guys get out of my office, get off my property and back into your cars. You go handle your problem. It has nothing to do with me."

They left.

Imperial Crane

John was happy to capitalize on the sensation, especially with the slowing economy.

> *"By 1994, we had two permanent bungee-jumping sites; one in Chicago and one in Arizona. At the peak of the venture, both sites served over eight hundred people per weekend. On average, each jumper would spend $130, bringing our gross for the weekend to well over $100,000."*

> *"We took the craze across the country, all the way to Fort Myers Beach, Florida, elevating our creativity with hair-raising stunts. But as more people got into the business to reap its seemingly easy profits, people started getting hurt everywhere, magnifying liability concerns. Fortunately, we never had a lawsuit or any accidents." – Jeff Bohne*

> *"I spent a month in Arizona training the operators down there when it all started. The whole thing was a fun experience; we all made good money on it, but it was a fad."*

> *"The only time you lose money on a fad is when you're the last one doing it. When John thought the fad was over, it was time to close shop."*
>
> *- Rick Bohne*

Our Journey: By B.J. Bohne

Imperial Crane Sales

When it all ended, John asked Jeff, "What now? What do you want to do?"

"I want to sell cranes. I think I'm really good at that. I know I can do that," he shot back.

Thus began Imperial Crane Sales in 1995, established for the sole purpose of renting, buying and selling cranes. John would later appoint his son Lance to be president of this division along with Jeff Bohne as vice president; both of whom still hold those positions presently.

> "I've been through school, got my degrees, including an MBA, and have done a lot of crazy things to survive. I have always been a big believer in constantly moving and hustling for more and better; and that is how I met John Bohne. I first heard about him through my brother who worked with the operator's union. But everyone knew John. He was like the godfather of Chicago in the crane world. 'You need to come work for me, and get away from those bums,' he'd say. So as soon as I got fed up with my situation, I called. 'John, I think I can help you out a little bit. I am a crane operator myself, but have some real good connections in the business.' 'Well come, let's talk,' he said. A couple of hours later, we shook hands on a

Imperial Crane

deal. Thus began an incredible journey for me that has completely transformed my life." –Daryl Lutes, Operations Manager

Daryl hit the ground running, having previously worked as a crane operator for a competitor company at a refinery in Indiana. He went straight back there, introducing himself as the new salesman for Imperial Crane.

"I sold them on our fine equipment and safety record. 'Well, I know you Daryl,' Frank Tommanoff, the supervisor said, 'I'll give you a shot.' We started slow and suddenly, the refinery announced a $13 billion expansion. We were immediately in the throes of a major opportunity. At the height of our contract, I had over two hundred and seventy five operators working for me there."

"For years, I worked out of my truck, quarter- backing the entire multi-million dollar operation without assistants or secretaries. It was a great ride! I loved every moment of it. I remember John coming to me saying, 'Looks like you've found your niche, Daryl. Whatever you need, let me know. You keep going and I will buy the equipment.' And that is what we did. We kept expanding and growing. I was fortunate enough to bring in hundreds of millions of dollars in business."- Daryl Lutes

Our Journey: By B.J. Bohne

Currently, Imperial Crane has over one hundred cranes at one of their refineries, and this refinery has not experienced a better safety record since its inception seventy-four years ago.

Imperial Crane Sales continued to grow well beyond Illinois into Indiana and beyond. Today, the company has operations all over the USA. They rank among the top crane companies in the world, dealing in the USA for major brands such as Tadano, STROS, and Barko, as well as the new line of Sany crawler cranes, which range from fifty to one thousand tons.

Travel Tip:

Know When It Is Time to Change Course

Crazy Kelly

John seemed to attract people with winning ideas. He definitely had a nose for opportunity.

Next door to Imperial Crane's headquarters was JB Industrial, a company operated by a rambunctious, fast-talking whip named Kelly O'Brian. Kelly had most of his business tied into a very large construction company that suddenly went belly-up; in fact, its bankruptcy is still one of the largest in U.S. history. Suddenly, Kelly, hurting and desperate, reached out to John for help.

Imperial Crane

"John and I were having lunch with Kelly, who, still reeling from the financial ruination, was telling us about his water-blasting business. John motioned with his hand for him to stop talking and asked, 'Kelly, how much have you been making doing this?' 'Three to five million a year.'"

"John, visibly shocked, almost spilled his wine; he smelled an opportunity and wanted in on the pie." – Whitey

The following day, he was on the hunt for water-blasters. He reached out to his brother Jim who agreed to finance a couple of machines.

In a few weeks, JB Industrial was back in business. John and Kelly were making money; lots and lots of money. They became close. In fact, Kelly would become B.J.'s godfather.

Was John Bohne aggressively shrewd? You bet he was! On one occasion, he got approved for a $10 million loan from one of his regular banks. He negotiated a 10 percent interest rate, but didn't draw on it. Seemingly out of no-where, interest rates skyrocketed to over 20 percent.

John saw an opportunity: instead of returning the money, he withdrew all $10 million, invested it and made a bundle, despite the bank's pleas to renegotiate the terms.

Our Journey: By B.J. Bohne

<u>These Unions</u>

Speaking to a union representative, B.J. said, "Hey buddy, you really want to work this out with me because your next stop is my old man, and it will not go well for you there. Trust me, he's not as sensitive and understanding as I am; he'll probably hurt your feelings. So let's reach a win-win consensus now."

B.J. knew his father all too well, especially when it came to union negotiations. The proverbial good cop/bad cop scenario worked great for them, but, in general, John never got along with unions. He would send Bill Tierney to union meetings, saying, "I can't even be in the same room with those guys." He didn't quite understand why they treated him with what he called "disdain and animosity" while he was providing needed employment for their workers. He took it personally, and for years seemed to be engaged in an on-going battle with them.

One day, B.J. asked John, "Hey Dad, why this animosity with the unions? Maybe if we didn't take this hard-line approach with them, we might get along better."

John shrugged his shoulders and replied, "Hey, you think you can handle them, have at it!" B.J. set up a meeting with the unions, hoping to talk sensibly with them. To his complete

Imperial Crane

shock, the entire meeting was one-sided. Everything was about them and what they needed.

When he met John after the meeting, he confessed, "Dad, I couldn't have sat down with a more selfish group of one-way brats than those goons; everything was about them.

All they kept asking was, 'What are you going to do for us?' There was absolutely no reciprocating discussion on their part at all."

John asked, "Well, what do you think now?" "Hmm, you know what Dad," B.J. replied, "I think I like your approach better."

"I remember my father telling me, regarding the local union, 'Jim, don't you ever forget what 150 has done for you. By you having this union license, they have put you through school.' John, on the other hand, absolutely hated the unions, but he knew it wasn't a fight he should engage in. He knew which fights to pick – the ones he could win." – Jim Bohne

Jim and John were at a crane exhibition in Las Vegas when the president of the operator's union came to join them at their table. "John, are you gonna say hello?" asked Jim.

Our Journey: By B.J. Bohne

"We don't talk. He's a thief. He knows that I know he's a thief, so we have nothing to talk about," John responded, unapologetically. Everyone was stunned, especially since the union president was within earshot of the snide remark.

As it turned out, though, John was correct. Shortly afterward, the union president was investigated by the FBI for suspicious activity.

Cunning as John was, he was a man of integrity who never wanted to exploit anyone. This is one of the reasons he had such disdain for unions. To him, they often seemed like spineless bastards who misused their power and took advantage of people.

The relationship between Local 150, Operating Engineers Union, and Imperial Crane was often contentious, but there was and still is great mutual respect for what both stand for.

"John would always say to me," recalls Ron Selby Sr., "'you know what, (Union) 150 has been good to me and my family. The last thing I want to do is have conflict with them, but I need to do right by my company.'"

While they both had to maintain a tough front in order to protect their separate interests, they cared deeply about the operators and always worked to make the men, the union and Imperial Crane successful; and still do today.

Imperial Crane

In fact, at the time of this writing, B.J. recently flew back from an appreciation gala where the union made a sizable donation to one of the charities he supports.

"Over the years, we have had to take hard positions in our negotiations with the unions. But at the end of the day, we come together and lock arms for our mutual betterment. Keep in mind that Grandpa Art was a union operator for fifty years; Dad was in the union for forty years; I have been in the union for twenty-five years. It is a fact that for three generations, unions have provided a source of income for our family that we could otherwise never have had as non-union crane operators." - B.J.

The Man Drives A Hard Bargain

"One day, I sold a crane we had owned for twenty years. We made over $3 million with it. It had served us very well, seeing we had paid $550,000 for it. I sold it for $650,000, making a $100,000 profit. When I told John, he stood up and threw a fit. 'You what? That was way cheap. That crane was worth $750,000.' He was livid. I got frustrated and told him, 'This is stupid. Here's what I'll do. I know the guy personally, he's an old friend. I'll send his deposit back and tell him you pulled the plug on this, and he'll be fine. That will take care of it.' I expected that would end the matter."

Our Journey: By B.J. Bohne

"Calmly, he responded, 'Well, no, you can't do that. A deal is a deal. You gave the guy your word, so you can't break it.' He was in a bind because of his ethics. He wanted the extra cash, but not at the expense of his integrity, despite the exit plan I laid out."

– Bill Tierney

• • •

Travel Tip:

Your Word is Your Bond. Lose That and You've Got Nothing

"John's reputation as a cold, hard businessman followed him. You could feel it by standing next to him. He carried an inexplicable aura of confidence. When he sat behind that desk, boy, he was like a king!" – Pat Walsh, remembering the first time he met John

• • •

"My dad passed away when I was ten. Immediately, Ron Selby, whose brother was part owner of Imperial Crane at the time, took me under his wing. So I grew up around the crane business, and couldn't wait to get my license as soon as I turned eighteen."

"I remember when I first met John as if it were yesterday. He was a scary figure to me. He was a man of very few words which, to me, made him all the more intimidating. When he walked into a room, everyone

Imperial Crane

stood up straight. He carried an imposing aura of authority." – Robert Kaleta, friend of B.J.

"John was a mythical figure to those who didn't know him. When he pulled his Mercedes into the garage, that meant whoever was closest to the car was responsible for getting it washed. He acted as though he was fifteen feet tall. So, of course, he was intimidating; maybe even scary. But there was a tender side to him. Maybe he wanted it that way." – Ron Selby Jr.

● ● ●

Travel Tips:

Never Invest Where You Have No Control

● ● ●

"Whereas many people were terrified of him, I really wasn't. Being best friends with his son Jonathan Bohne, I really wasn't afraid. I was the twelve-year-old kid who would start a conversation about football, golf; anything. I think he indulged me because I was not stressful to him. He was soft-spoken, but always meant business. If you never took the time to actually break the ice, you never got to know John Bohne." – Fred Hunssinger

Whether it was insurance, real estate or cranes, he always made sure he had a significant say. And whenever he got involved in ventures where he had little or no say, he lost money. Time and time again, he would get slam-dunk, no–brainer opportunities with promise for quick returns or turna-

Our Journey: By B.J. Bohne

round. Every time he got involved in a deal that, however promising, went against his better instinct, somehow his share of the proposition would die on the vine. B.J. saw that principle lived out so much in front of him that he jokes about this experience.

"Jeff wanted to go bet on horses one day so he and I went to the track to let off some steam after a very long day's work. The problem was I had no clue about betting on horses. I told Jeff, 'Let's keep it simple. You pick two horses and bet one hundred dollars for each of us.' Three hours later, Jeff returned shouting victory, 'I won! I won!' So I said, 'Great, if you won, I must have won as well, yes?' Jeff said, 'Not really. Sure, I bet one hundred dollars for both of us, but the problem is, that's not the ticket that won."

"See, I found another three dollars and bought a separate ticket, and that's what won.' He had won $3000. So I learned this lesson first hand: put your money where you have control. Imperial Crane will buy a crane today and get it paid off in ten years, at which time it will be worth more than what we bought it for. Meanwhile, it has generated multiple times more money than its book value. Right here, I have an asset that I completely understand and can touch. So, when people give me all those flowery, get-rich-quick opportunities, I tell them, 'Thanks, but no thanks. I know

Imperial Crane

cranes. I do cranes. I can see and touch my cranes, and I make money on cranes.'" – B.J.

I'll Give You Ten Grand To Disappear

Although John loved Gayle, the trappings of success brought considerable pressure to their marriage. As committed as he knew he needed to be to his wife and family, his appetite for the proverbial hunt seemed unquenchable.

By the time B.J. announced he wanted to get married, his father's scars and history had completely affected his view on marriage as an institution. To see his son walking down the same road of pain and disappointment seemed unbearable.

"I remember having dinner with John and five mutual friends in downtown Chicago one evening. Earlier that night, three of us had announced we were getting remarried – yup, a second go 'round. After staring the intended grooms down for a few minutes, John said, 'What on earth do you think you are doing?' And he went on to give a long morose prognosis of each of their marriages." – Sam Palumbo

Strong as he was, he really couldn't stop his own son B.J. from getting married to his crush, Crystle.

Our Journey: By B.J. Bohne

"After badgering me for weeks with no real success, Dad knew he had one more shot: the wedding. He showed up in his black tuxedo, wearing his big cowboy hat, Bolero Western tie, and cowboy boots. Talk about total defiance; he wanted to make a statement! In a last ditch effort, he went to the minister and promised to pay him $10,000 if he would disappear. Of course, the minister declined his generous offer." –B.J.

Jim recalls John's exact words that day, "Look, as far as I am concerned, I would rather pay ten grand now, than one hundred grand six months from now."

And to his credit, John was right.

"I don't begrudge my old man for whatever he did. Deep down in his heart, he was genuinely concerned for my future and well being. He had been married and it hadn't worked out like he had hoped. Dad was trying to protect me from the pain of marital shipwreck he had endured." – B.J.

Only four months later, B.J. realized the marriage wasn't going to make it. He and John were at a convention in San Antonio, Texas, and B.J. was completely devastated. He told his father:

"Dad, I need to get out."

Imperial Crane

"No problem, we'll take care of this." John replied.

What? Really? No lecture or a long I-told-you-so talk? B.J. was shocked his father didn't say anything about his obviously wrong choice of a mate. He was right after all. The marriage was a disaster. They were not adequately prepared for the immense commitment.

John didn't waste time rehashing mistakes; why do that? He was solution-minded. After comforting his broken-hearted son, John called his divorce attorney, Rico, and scheduled a 7:00 a.m. meeting that following Monday.

In eight days, B.J. was standing in front of a judge. Once again, Dad had taken care of it. Fortunately, B.J. and Crystle remain close friends today.

Working together through this immensely painful episode tremendously helped John and B.J.'s relationship to grow. Whether John felt deep regret which he could now share with his son; guilt for not protecting B.J. from the hurtful decision in the first place; or remorse for the times he failed to step up and be an emotionally supportive father, this experience helped strengthen their bond.

"For whatever reason, we seemed glued to the hip after my short marriage ended. We were together almost every night, meeting clients or simply hanging out. We played golf almost every day. Our relationship

Our Journey: By B.J. Bohne

definitely changed. He also eased up on me as far as business performance expectations were concerned. In fact, he purposely involved me more in the directional decisions of the company. I remember those moments fondly to this day." – B.J.

"Spending six hours a day on the green with his father helped the two of them get connected. No matter what kind of childhood he had, that definitely helped." – Jim Bohne

It was not very long after this period that John passed away. Looking back, it appears as though the reconnection efforts were his way of silently saying farewell.

The Sheriff

John was a deputy sheriff of Cook and Will Counties in Illinois. He owned a helicopter and a Cessna airplane.

"Running late for a game? We never had any problems. Here was my dad driving down the shoulder of the freeway past everyone. It was cool! One day I got into a fight with a group of kids from my high school. We got arrested and booked."

"'Your father is here to pick you up,' the officer announced. 'You didn't tell us he is a Cook County sher-

Imperial Crane

iff.' I hadn't said anything because I thought Dad would hit the wall."

"'So you know what we are going to do? We are not charging you with anything. We are going to release you to him. I am sure he will take good care of it.' Thankfully, Dad was cool about it." – B.J.

One day, while John was driving from Palm Springs, California to Phoenix, Arizona, he was pulled over by a state trooper for doing over 120 m.p.h. When he flashed his badge, the officer asked, "Well, what do you do for the force?"

"I am a pilot."

"Well, next time keep the flying in the air."

Quintessential John

"One thing John was good at was rolling the dice. We all stood by and watched him do the craziest things, and consequently succeed right in front of us. He was very courageous. When it was time to do the hard things, John didn't show any feelings; and he was never afraid to call anyone's bluff." – Whitey

Our Journey: By B.J. Bohne

One day Whitey and John were out drinking, relaxing after a hard week of work. Whitey had their week's take right in his front pocket – a check for a cool $400,000.

A guy was mouthing off at the bar and John said to Whitey, "Hey, got that check? Hand it to me." He took it and threw it on the counter and said, "Here's mine. Put yours down. If you've really got any guts, let's flip a coin for the whole lot." The two stared each other down for what seemed an eternity, and, of course, the loudmouth recoiled. As they walked away, Whitey was dumbfounded; he couldn't believe John's courage. Was he bluffing? Of course not, but how could he stake so much on a silly bet?

"We were at the bank one day, and John came out with a heavy bag. As we arrived at the job site, John got out of the car to look around. He said to me, 'Hey, sorta keep an eye on the car.' 'Keep an eye on the car? Why?' I asked. 'Cause I got $1.5 mil in that bag right there.' My jaw dropped. Who drives around with a million bucks in the trunk of his car?" – Whitey

But that was quintessential John Bohne.

"John, Lance, B.J, Jeff, Bill, Bob and I were celebrating the signing of a big contract with Tadano, a major Japanese crane distributor. About ninety minutes into dinner, one of our Japanese counterparts decided to

Imperial Crane

make a toast." He said, 'This is wonderful – Japanese and Americans doing business together. But going back in history, things weren't always like this. We have a question to ask of you: why did you drop two bombs on us?' And without missing a beat John replied, 'Because we didn't have a third!' Everyone's jaw dropped. Who comes up with that kind of stuff?" – Ron Selby Jr.

Did John trivialize money? Was it unimportant to him? By no means.

"I remember this one fella who lived in a very rough Chicago neighborhood and owed us quite a bit of money. No one wanted to collect from him in that part of town; I, too, was concerned. 'Whitey, don't sweat it. I've got this,' John assured me. As we got into the car, he pointed to a black bag next to me. 'In that bag back there is your shotgun. I'll use this revolver. That should work in case anything happens. Let's go!'"

"With that firepower, we braved that neighborhood to pick up our money. We got the cash, and got out without a scratch; thank God. One thing we were always proud of was that we never lost money. We always collected what was owed us." – Whitey

Our Journey: By B.J. Bohne

As much as he rolled the dice to take jaw-dropping risks, he was not impulsive. "I remember him and my brother Bill meticulously researching the cranes before we bought them," recalls John Tierney. For hours they would carefully work the numbers, dimensions, capacities, and so on, together. John absolutely hated conjecture; he had to have the raw facts. Once the purchase made sense, the decision was made quickly and with finality.

It's Not Just About The Money

Yes, John valued money; some thought perhaps he valued it a bit too much. "A lot of people would say he had fishhooks in his pockets," says John Tierney, "But when it was time to do something, he stepped up right away." He liked to go to Dunlap's, his favorite restaurant, but the waitresses were terrified of him!

He was particular; very particular. When he asked for a twist of lemon, he did not want a wedge of lemon, and he was sure to let the waitresses know if they got it wrong.

"We were on our way to Germany one time and were sitting in business class. The flight attendant came to take our meal order, and one of the choices was steak. John said, 'I want it medium rare.' We tried to explain to him that the meals were pre-cooked, and he couldn't order it to the temperature he wanted.

Imperial Crane

She brought out the steak and, of course, it was not medium rare. John had a fit! Fortunately, for the flight attendant, we were all on her side." – Karen Vulcani, an old friend

"Flying with him was a challenge. He never learned to respect the degenerating culture of the airlines, which resulted in less personal interaction and service; he thought things should have remained as they were in the 1980s when stewardesses did everything they could to make the passengers happy. So many times, they wanted to call the police on him. He would promptly pull out his badge and say, 'Here, I am the police!' To him, service kept getting worse and worse as the flight attendants became more and more empowered." – B.J.

On one particular long-haul flight, a lady passenger happened to be chain-smoking. Becoming irritated, John said, "Hey lady, will you please lighten up a bit with that? You're killing us back here."

She replied, "Hey, I can do whatever I want," and promptly lit up another cigarette.

Taking his cue, John nonchalantly threw an airline blanket over her, causing her to scream in shock. The flight attendant ran up the row, bewildered. "Sorry, it's me." John

Our Journey: By B.J. Bohne

admitted, "I thought she was on fire." Everyone roared with laughter!

> *"We were in Acapulco at the Paradise Club one day when John announced, 'I want to go swim with the dolphins.' He promptly disrobed and jumped into the pool with the dolphins. Alarmed, security demanded he immediately get out of the water. John's response? 'Maybe you should have built a higher fence.'" – Jim Bohne*

B.J. tells another story of a customer who owed *Imperial Crane* quite a bit of money. When Bill Tierney cut off his credit line, the customer approached John, "Look, you don't know me, but I need credit from you for a big job coming up. I know I owe you guys already, but this job will more than make up for whatever I owe you, plus so much more."

John was persuaded, primarily because they were members of the same golf club, Midlothian, and he convinced Bill to extend the guy more credit.

Shortly thereafter, the customer declared bankruptcy protection and *Imperial Crane* couldn't collect on any money, including the old debt. Obviously, he knew he was going under before he asked *Imperial Crane* for the credit.

Imperial Crane

Meanwhile, he still went to the golf club and continued to finance his lifestyle through other companies; clearly a ploy. What bothered John more than anything else was the flagrancy of his behavior; he took advantage of his kindness and status with Midlothian Country Club.

People still talk about what John did next. He got the directory for the entire golf club membership and sent everyone a note, saying: **Jim needs help. Anyone willing to contribute please send $1 to this address**. The guy was humiliated and sued John. He won the case and John was fined one dollar.

Was money important to him? Sure it was, but only as a means to freedom, access, growth, and more cranes.

"I was out on a job one day and needed some chains. So I called the office and John answered. 'Okay, let me run them out to you right now,' he said. So he pulled up at the site in a brand new Cadillac Eldorado. He walked up to the crane and I asked, 'You've got somebody bringing the chains out to me?' He says, 'No, they are in the car.' So I asked him to pop the trunk. He said, 'No, they are in the back seat!' I was dumbfounded. 'In the back seat? You put rusty chains in the back seat? Why didn't you throw them in a truck?' He said, 'That's my truck. Don't worry about the seats. We make enough money, I will buy

Our Journey: By B.J. Bohne

another car!' That was his attitude – you work hard and you play hard!" - Ron Selby Sr.

If he was not in the office, or out dining with clients, you could find him at Chicago's most celebrated private golf course, the Butler National Golf Club.

"I found this Bonanza airplane at a killer deal; I think it was $14,000. Well, I later found out why it was such a deal. Most of the Bonanzas had a habit of losing their v-tails upon takeoff. We decided to fly this plane to Florida to visit with some of Gayle's friends and landed in a cornfield. When we took off, Gayle and the girls were signaling at us, yelling at the top of their voices. We had corn stacks stuck all through the plane's tail. It's a miracle we didn't crash." – Jim Bohne

As his net worth grew, John would later buy a helicopter and an airplane to transport clients, attend workshops and close multi-million dollar deals up and down the country. He enjoyed ski trips and vacations all over the world with his friends and family.

"A lot of people never knew him at all. If he liked you, he liked you. If he didn't, you were just outta luck. Those who didn't know him thought him a heartless, cold businessman. I was fortunate to get close enough to know the real John. I remember traveling to our an-

Imperial Crane

nual crane expo out in Vegas one year. This was like the big deal event for crane guys. While other participants were riding shuttles, carpooling and eating hot dogs in the parking lot, we were riding limos and enjoying lobster."

"That stood out to me, not because we were spending more money, but because John Bohne strongly believed in living life to the fullest!"
- Daryl Lutes

Travel Tip:

Surround Yourself With The Right People

"One day I asked John to teach me the business. He answered, 'Sure I will teach you everything I know, but I will never teach you how to do banks.' Well, at first I didn't get it, but everyone around knew that financing was John's specialty. He knew how to get loans, negotiate rates and leverage equity like no one else."

"Then I got it, and his response was pretty telling: 'I will teach you how to do everything I do, but not enough to replace me.'"

"He believed that the best leaders hire people who are smart enough - maybe smart enough to run the business, but not smart enough to own it." – Whitey

Our Journey: By B.J. Bohne

That might explain the incredible loyalty found at *Imperial Crane* today. This is one company that doesn't have internal vultures circling the place.

Chapter Travel Tips

#17: If You're Gonna Do Something, You'd Better Do It Right

This travel tip deals with excellence. What is excellence? My simple definition is: Staying One Step Ahead of Ordinary. It's doing a common thing in an uncommon way. Like bungee jumping. For John, good enough was simply unacceptable. Industrialist Andrew Carnegie concluded, "There are two types of people who never achieve much in their lifetime: the person who won't do what he is told, and the person who does no more than he is told."

#18: Know When It Is Time To Change Course

It is a fact that every stage of development is to be celebrated and enjoyed, and then outgrown. Sure, change is frightening, uncertain, uncomfortable and downright dangerous sometimes, but without it there cannot be growth. So, as good as it is to know when to jump into something, it's equally important to know when to exit. Think about Xerox, Blockbuster and other major corporations that missed their windows of change. Imperial Crane watches the trends and constantly keeps re-tooling for greater productivity. Failure to do that could mean its demise.

Our Journey: By B.J. Bohne

#19: Your Word is Your Bond. Lose That And You Have Nothing

B.J. has told me multiple times, "Dr. Dennis, my dad had more integrity than anyone I know." How powerful. The word integrity originates from the Latin word 'integer', which means inner strength. Integrity is the absence of duplicity. People of integrity are reliable and accountable. Unfortunately, this is a vanishing trait today. An Italian proverb says, "Between saying and doing, many a pair of shoes is worn out." No matter how well-meaning people are, they are what they do not what they say. Always listen with your eyes, not your ears. Integrity means real believability which, like it or not, is much more than mere words or rhetoric. This is critical to any partnership, be it business or marriage. Here is a verse to ponder: "The man of integrity walks securely, but he who takes crooked paths will be found out" (Proverbs 10:9 NIV).

#20: Never Invest Where You Have No Control

Little needs to be said about this travel tip. We have all heard the admonition that you should avoid investing in places you don't really understand. The Bohnes take it a step further. They insist that not only is it important to put your money into a vehicle you understand, but it's important that you have firm control of that vehicle as well. The Bohnes know cranes. They invest in cranes. They make money in cranes. Period.

#21: Surround Yourself With The Right People

I have devoted many years to studying this subject. Simply put, you don't have the time to live your life, make mistakes, learn from those mistakes, and then implement the lessons

Imperial Crane

you've learned. In order to live to their full potential, wise people learn how to read the lives of those who have gone ahead of them. They are a living witness to the folly or wisdom of a particular decision. The Book of Proverbs says, "He that walks with wise men shall be wise: but a companion of fools shall be destroyed (Proverbs 13:20 KJV). At the dusk of their lives, most achievers will tell you that if they could do it over again, they would pour their lives into the right relationships. Yes, relationships are challenging, but also consequential and extremely critical.

But I Don't Care

It's raining today like torrents you'd say – but I don't care,
For it's not raining everywhere.

Someone frowned at me today – but I don't care,
For I get lots of smiles everywhere.

I get dirty when I garden – but I don't care,
For soon I have flowers everywhere.

I have weeds come up here and there – but I don't care,
For some have seeds for birds to share.

And sometimes I even get a plant quite rare.
I have no car to go anywhere – but I don't care,

For many friends take me everywhere.

Willadene
The Master's Treasures
Copyright 2000

Chapter 6

John's Friends

"Without a doubt, John was a man's man!"
– Jeremy Roenick

"John, I am broke. I think I want to come back to work," Whitey said, almost sure John would hang up on him. He had walked off a job site, abandoned the crane – their only crane – and driven out of state to Colorado. After spending every penny he had, he was ready to face his folly and pay for his stupidity.

But to his shock, John replied, "Alright, I will get you some money down there. You get yourself back here and get right back to work." He never reprimanded him or mentioned the incident again.

You Never Had To Wonder

That was not the first time Whitey had walked off a job site.

Our Journey: By B.J. Bohne

"We had just bought our first crane. As I was booming the crane in a blind spot one day, disaster struck. The load over-swung and cut a building in half. I panicked. So I kicked the window out and literally took off, leaving the site and abandoning the crane. When John heard about it, he looked me up and found me. By then, I was thinking, 'This is it for me. I am done with the crane business.' So I told him, 'John, it's over for me, man – too dangerous.' I was yelling, but John replied in a calm, disarming voice, 'Don't worry about it. Let's go take care of it.' Somehow, I believed him, and we did take care of it." – Whitey

Throughout those very stressful early days, John and Whitey fought all the time. He told me he must have quit a hundred times, but even when he jumped ship to go work for a competitor, there was still room for him with John if he chose to return.

"Whenever I needed something, I'd call. John was a loyal friend, and boy do I miss that!" – Whitey

Loyalty; that's what this chapter is about. In researching this book, I had the privilege of spending many hours with John's family, his close friends and associates.

One thing that prominently resonated throughout our conversations was his sense of commitment and loyalty.

Imperial Crane

He was not a man with many friends. Although he was hugely popular, magnetic, imposing and even charismatic at times, John really only confided in a few people; but once he let you in, you were in.

"I remember bumping into him one time in the early 90s. We hadn't really seen each other, or even talked in a couple of years. But, predictably, our conversation led to golf; John loved golf. I told him about my plans to join Butler National Golf Club. Without hesitation, he offered to write a recommendation letter and sponsor me; that is, after making me promise we would get together and play golf monthly. Was John loyal? Absolutely! Once a friendship was established with him that was it. You never had to wonder."

– Sam Palumbo

Travel Tip:

Real Friends Don't Need To Keep Doing The Honeymoon Dance

"My wife and I wanted to fly out to Las Vegas to renew our wedding vows. I asked John if he knew someone out there we could connect with. He said he'd get back to me. I booked our hotel, but when we got there, John had arranged an upgrade to the honeymoon suite with bouquets of flowers all over the place. The place looked kingly. He also organized a stretch limousine to take us wherever we wanted to

Our Journey: By B.J. Bohne

*go. As if that wasn't enough, he got us premium tick-
ets to shows all over town. One evening; we were tak-
en to the front of the auditorium. We had no clue who
was performing that night. Suddenly, Sting, the
Grammy award-winning superstar, came out with personal greetings for us on our wedding. We were blown
away. Well, that was John! I will never forget the
man."- Daryl Lutes*

You Are Either In Or Out

Local 150, one of the main worker's unions in this part of
the country, was on strike with picket lines on *Imperial
Crane's* premises. John noticed some of his staff were also
out there picketing, and he was livid. He felt betrayed and
slapped in the face. He asked for the names of staff members who were involved, and as he read the list, he began to
recount their stories. "I can't believe this guy is out there. Oh,
and this guy here, I got him his union card, got him a life, and
now he is out there picketing me?"

Once the strike was over he fired them all; even some of
his long-time friends. For John, loyalty meant steadfastness in
commitment. Because he was loyal, he expected the same
from those he had around him.

*"One year, we went through this huge expansion.
Well, it was huge at the time; we grew from seven to
twenty-five cranes. Our credit lines were maxed and*

Imperial Crane

every cent was spent before we made it. It was Christmas time, and John came up to me with this huge end-of-year bonus. I was blown away. 'John, we can't afford this,' I protested. His response was, 'Bill, understand this. The shareholders - and that's me - really don't give a rip. We might go broke doing it, but there is no argument about this: we will work hard, but we'll also enjoy ourselves doing it.' He laughed as he walked away." – Bill Tierney

Without a doubt, John was unpredictable. Some might call him eccentric, maybe sometimes even erratic and rough. From a distance, he often acted as though he didn't care much about anyone, but those who were close to him have a far different story. Underneath that hard shell was a caring man who often bent over backwards for others.

"One day, an employee who had been with us for years figured he could fill up his truck with gas on the company dime. Well, he got caught. When he came in to procure his paycheck for the week, he was told John wanted to talk to him in his office. They stepped outside and John told him, 'Two choices: I could rip up your paycheck because you have stolen from me; or you pay me back for the gas, promise you won't do this again, I'll give you your check and we forget this ever happened.' He chose option two, and ever since

Our Journey: By B.J. Bohne

then has been one of the straightest employees this company has ever had." – John Tierney

"I remember the day I quit college. The first thing I did was come to John. He was like a father to me. My life seemed bleak and hopeless at the time. After listening to my woes, he said, 'You will be fine. Regardless what happened at school, you can count on me. You will always have a job here.' This gave me so much peace."

"And yeah, many years later, I am still here. Having started as a shop worker, doing everything you can imagine, I now hold one of this company's most important positions – all because of John's loyalty." – Fred Hunssinger

John often ran to the aid of alcoholics, drug dependents and the destitute. He helped so many people. If you had a good idea, and got it to him, he was ready to get behind you.

"My brother was a great man. You could not have a friend more loyal than John. He had five or six good friends. Outside of that, he had business acquaintances that trusted his judgment. Then he had ties with associations that he regularly and faithfully worked

Imperial Crane

with. Aside from that, he didn't care what anyone else thought about him." –Jim Bohne

This is one character trait that strikes me as most admirable about John Bohne. Indeed, he had friends and, naturally, he cared what those friends thought about him; but only to an extent. As vulnerable as he might have been, he never left himself open to the whims of opinion. For example, Bill Tierney, his vice president, will tell you that John did value his opinion very much, but not to the point where he was imprisoned by it. It seems to me that John Bohne was at peace within himself. He was confident in his decisions, tastes, and opinions and regardless what anyone thought, he was going to do what he felt he needed to do. Period.

Travel Tip:

Everyone Has An Opinion. Pick Your Circle of Counsel And Ignore the Rest.

Loyal To A Fault

"A helicopter landed in our yard here at the office one day; it was here to pick John up. Hours later, he came back, but he seemed troubled. We learned that he had been offered a partnership position in Chicago's first casino, a proposition worth millions of dollars. He was supposed to be happy, but he wasn't.

189

Our Journey: By B.J. Bohne

Why? His old friend, Mayor Daley, was vehemently opposed to the casino. He chose to walk away from the million dollar opportunity so he wouldn't betray his friendship with Daley." – John Tierney

Jim Gedmin, one of his old friends, told me, "If you kept your mouth shut about his business, John was faithful and very loyal. He took care of you, no matter what."

"Without a doubt, Dad's most treasured investments were his deep relationships; to this day, I continue to benefit from them. Recently, I had to make a case before our village board of trustees for a variance on my property in Oakbrook. Getting anything like that done is no easy accomplishment, this being one of Chicago's finest suburbs."

"I showed up a bit anxious, but ready to make my case. Right before the meeting, one of the trustees came to me and said, 'Don't worry about tonight. You will be okay. We have a mutual friend who knew your father really well. He was a great man.' I'm happy to say, my variance was approved." – B.J.

Conversely, when you got on John's bad side, you were in for the fight of your life. Says John Tierney, "We stayed out of his way; never asked questions that had nothing to do

Imperial Crane

with us. If we needed to know something, we knew he would let us know."

"We were at a golf club one day and this guy came out to ask if John would play a round of golf with him. With his back turned to him, he said, 'No, I won't play golf with you today. I will not play with you tomorrow. I will never play with you even if you were the only person left in the world.' We were shocked at the time, but it turned out this guy was a manipulating freeloader who had stiffed John in a deal once before. If you were on John's bad list, watch out!" – Jim Bohne

The Trouble With Kelly

"This Kelly is too volatile," observed John, "I'm afraid of what he could do to us. He's spending more than he makes. We gotta be careful here." John's partnership with his water-blasting buddy had become worrisome to him. Sure, they were making money, but the exotic playboy parties, fantastical European excursions and splashy, over-the-top vacations were alarming.

"Kelly was lots of fun. I will never forget this one time when he chartered a super luxury boat on Lake Michigan, and filled it with beautiful women and cases of Dom Perignon. Yup, those were fun times; but come to think of it, he was also a bad influence.

Our Journey: By B.J. Bohne

Those constant parties sure took a toll on our personal lives, including our marriages; eventually ending mine. Now, don't get me wrong, we made the choices, but it was that partying environment that created the options." – Jim Bohne

● ● ●

Travel Tip:

The Company You Keep Will Ultimately Influence Your Values

● ● ●

JB Industrial was in trouble. John and Jim could no longer draw any remuneration because the company was running out of money; Kelly had spent it all. Eventually, he declared bankruptcy and the party was over.

Out of desperation, he came to John one day and said, "If you don't give me some cash, I am turning you in." John was befuddled. Here was a guy who, only a few months ago had come to him crying with his back completely against the wall. Now he was blackmailing him?

For some time, John had purchased his cranes and water-blasting machines in Michigan, effectively avoiding Illinois taxes. His attorneys didn't see a problem with this, so he never gave it much thought, until Kelly threatened to use that to extort money from him.

Imperial Crane

"Well, Kelly, you do what you gotta do. I ain't giving you a cent." John challenged. Within a few weeks, John was subpoenaed for tax evasion.

The Lawsuit

As the investigation began, John got a curious visit from the FBI; they wanted to meet him. They claimed to have a proposition for him that would make the "tax thing" go away.

"Mr. John Bohne, we are aware of your tax issue, but that is not our concern. We are investigating Mayor Daley. We are aware of your political ties with him. You have served as his fundraising chairman and we think that's why he has awarded you contracts worth millions of dollars. But we are not after you. Just give us everything you know about him and we'll leave you alone."

Without skipping a beat, John shot back, "Indeed, the mayor and I have enjoyed a thirty-year relationship. We go way back. He is my friend."

"I completely resent and reject your insinuations about our company and our business ethics. Imperial Crane legitimately bids for all our contracts, and aside from that, I have nothing to give you. He is a good man. Now if you will kindly get out of my office . . ."

Our Journey: By B.J. Bohne

In an effort to intimidate him, they flipped back their coats to show off their guns and badges. John reached into his drawer, picked up his own gun and badge, and slammed them on top of the desk. He said, "Well, here is my badge and here is my gun. So what are you going to do?" You could hear a pin drop. They left.

> *"Dad never went to college, and because of that he made doubly sure to hire the very best accountants. In fact, he did this in every area of his life: he had the top attorneys, administrators and professionals, period. All his T's were crossed no matter what. He knew he was innocent, and was not about to be intimidated by anyone, whether it was the Internal Revenue Service or the FBI." – B.J.*

John decided to fight.

Ordinarily, if the government thinks you owe taxes, they simply make their case. If it was a discrepancy, as they had originally claimed, they should have simply asked him to pay.

This was a civil matter, which is what the first judge said before he dismissed the case. But since John was charged criminally, he knew this was not about back taxes.

They were blackmailing him for information they thought he had.

Imperial Crane

The government spent millions of dollars trying to tie him to illegal deals, but they failed. Eventually, they appealed to the State of Illinois Supreme Court, which also threw the case out, fully exonerating John and Imperial Crane.

"I asked Dad one day 'Was this worth it? Seven long years of investigations, media attacks, stress, and all the money? Was your loyalty worth it?' Hesitatingly, he replied, 'I think so. Yes, it was.' After all that, Dad still thought loyalty was important, no matter what it cost."

Travel Tip:

True Friends Will Walk With You Even If It Is Inconvenient

"I will tell you now that even if he had anything on Mayor Daley, and I am not suggesting he did by any means, no matter what the government or anyone else, for that matter, did, they were not going to get anywhere with him. His loyalty meant a lot more than status." – B.J.

When the dust settled on his lawsuit, John felt vindictive; he wanted to get back at the man responsible for his failed prosecution; the man who, at the time, happened to be running for Governor of Illinois. With his vast resources, John got full-throttle behind the prospective Governor's opponent, eventually getting him elected.

Our Journey: By B.J. Bohne

To this day, B.J. believes the tremendous stress of that lawsuit took a toll on his father's health to the point of possibly triggering the health challenges that ensued.

Health Challenges

"I think I better go to the emergency room," John announced to Gayle. Seeing as he had been up to his mischief again, Gayle wasn't amused and really didn't feel all that compassionate. She took him to Blue Island Hospital, but "I was tempted to take him the long way, just to punish him," Gayle admits.

In the emergency room, John was diagnosed with clogged arteries and immediately admitted to the hospital. He had a family history of heart problems and his own triple bypass surgery twenty years earlier had precipitated a history of coronary issues. Even then, those around him knew his latest problems were stress related.

> "As John was being rushed to the operating room for his bypass surgery, he was trying to get my attention. I hurriedly leaned in to listen, thinking maybe my husband had some sweet assuring words to say to me before he was put under."
>
> "'Gayle, please call Vince and let him know I will not be able to meet him for golf tomorrow.' 'What? What

Imperial Crane

a waste! Is that all you have to say to me?' I replied. I wanted to slam the gurney into the wall."

– Gayle Bohne

From Bad To Worse

"We were at dinner one night in May of 2003 and noticed that Dad's eyes were yellow; we thought it was jaundice. A couple of days later, he scheduled a visit to go see his doctor for a checkup. Initially, they thought it had to do with his gall bladder, but after they did a thorough examination, they discovered a tumor on his liver. I still remember when he broke the news to us. He said rather nonchalantly, 'Okay guys, when I had my gall bladder thing, they found a tumor. It's no problem. They are going to do a procedure in June. They will get in there and tie off the infected section, cut off circulation and, being that the liver is one of those organs that can rejuvenate itself; the healthy part of my liver will grow stronger and healthier. Ninety days later, they'll just cut off the infected part.'" – B.J.

It was during that sixty to ninety-day period that John completely lived it up. He had a most remarkable summer, going out almost every night. He won the A-Club Championship at the Midlothian Country Club.

Our Journey: By B.J. Bohne

Ironically, he seemed to be in the absolute best shape of his life. "Dad hadn't touched a drink in four months. Without exaggeration, it was the healthiest I'd ever seen him in twenty years," said B.J.

> *"Dad and I would sometimes golf together and quite often, he and I would get paired together in high-stakes tournaments. I remember after we had won a big tournament, he calmly told me about how bad things were. Things went down so fast after that; one day we were out golfing and the next, it seemed, he was losing weight and deteriorating fast." – Lance*

"Jim, I gotta tell you something," John announced to his twin brother. "I went in for a regular check-up a couple of weeks ago, and the doctors found a tumor on my liver. They say it's cancerous."

Those shocking words resonated painfully at one of the family's most vulnerable and painful moments – their sister Jane's funeral.

They had just lost an incredible woman whom B.J. knew as his beloved godmother.

Maybe it was the somberness of that August moment in 2003 that prompted John to confess the feebleness of his

Imperial Crane

own existence. Unbeknownst to him and everyone else, the cancer had already metastasized.

"It's after they went to try and remove it that they realized it had spread to his lungs. So, removing part of his liver wouldn't do any good." – B.J.

"When Bill first told me about John's cancer, I was shocked. We all hoped the best for him, but you could tell he wasn't doing well; he started to weaken noticeably. I worried about him. Being last to leave the office, I would often find him working long after everyone else had left. I'd ask if he needed help, and his answer was always the same, 'No, John, I'm fine.' This was a guy who was constantly concerned about his cranes, but never complained about his health or well-being." – John Tierney

Over the next few months, the doctors tried to synthesize a treatment regiment for John, but failed. Because of his heart history and his age, they couldn't operate; they couldn't do anything for him.

"Dad would spend hours and hours on the phone with cancer experts. I remember getting frustrated with him on the golf course when he had to make these calls. He tried to get into trial cancer research programs all over Illinois, Florida, and Texas, but no specialist would

Our Journey: By B.J. Bohne

take him or even see him. Ironically, they were looking for healthier patients for their test studies. Besides, they said that the cancer had become too advanced for any of those programs." – B.J.

Gayle prayed for John several times a day, asking God for his healing. A few months earlier, John had suddenly filed for divorce, something that had shocked everyone who knew him. Although their marriage was far from buoyant, the two seemed to have lived amicably for decades. But now he wanted to settle down and maybe atone for some of his mistakes. He had moved into a condo downtown, and it was as though he was dating Gayle again. They had become very close.

"After his divorce, he seemed to settle down. He became a much calmer guy. I think he even got closer to God, as he started to regularly attend mass. 'I can't continue living this double life' he would say. 'I really need to straighten out, to make things right.'" – Jim Bohne

"John was in the process of building a house for Gayle. While I was there helping out one afternoon, she told me about John's worsening condition, and how the doctors here had failed to treat him. I knew if there was anything out there in the world that could

Imperial Crane

make a difference, John was going to try and find it. That was the kind of man he was." – Fred Hunssinger

Munich

A family friend and golfing buddy, Vince Alegra, talked to John about a cutting-edge cancer treatment facility in Germany. He had been told that celebrities such as Siegfried of Siegfried & Roy, the late Farrah Fawcett and a few other big names had been treated successfully at the famed Leonardo's Clinic in Munich. They prided themselves on having a very holistic approach to cancer treatment.

As a last ditch effort, John decided to give it a shot, especially since everyone else had pretty much given up. Prior to his departure, Jim remembered spending a weekend together up in their vacation home in Summit Lake, Wisconsin. John had made this stunning statement, "Jim, I don't get it. I really don't know how I can feel so good, and be so sick."

"I remember Vince and I going to pick him up the day he flew to Germany for the treatments. We had coffee and talked. He was very optimistic about the program; we all were. In fact, Vince knew someone personally whose cancer had been forced into remission from the treatments. John was well aware of the risks. Besides, when your doctors tell you they have run

Our Journey: By B.J. Bohne

out of options for you, what do you do? Nothing? John wasn't one of those guys who sat there waiting for his fate. He had to do something, and he really thought this would work. Whatever the case, he wanted it to work. He had to hope in something. I had watched my own father die within six weeks of being told there was no hope. Hope is important to our existence. It was clear that the option to go to this center in Germany gave John hope. Yeah, I celebrate him for loving life enough to try everything out there. It was a very interesting conversation that morning. It was almost as though he knew he was going. 'Sam, I have B.J. lined up for this; Lance and Jonathan are set up with that; and here is what I am leaving for Gayle.' I interrupted, 'John, look, you are coming right back. You'll be gone for a couple of weeks and they will take care of you.'" – Sam Palumbo

"'Look, I've got cancer,' John announced abruptly to me at the end of summer, 2003. 'I will be going to Germany to try some experimental stuff that hopefully will give me another two to three years.' That shocked me to the core." – Daryl Lutes

John flew to Munich and began his rigorous treatments. He would take long chilly walks after his daily regiments, at which time he'd call his family and friends. "It was not until much later that I received his whopping $7,000 phone bill from AT&T," recalls B.J., "Even while on these rigorous treat-

Imperial Crane

ments, Dad constantly kept in touch with us back here. He worked to the very end."

Each week, Vince and Sam sent him his favorite magazines, movies, and CDs. "He called me from the clinic one day," Gayle remembers, "and said, 'Gayle, I am going to be fine. There is this guy who has gone through the treatments and is fine now. His cancer is completely gone.'"

Travel Tip:

Only God Knows The Number of Our Days

"He really thought he could beat the cancer. He had so much on his docket to do, with projects planned and meetings scheduled. He definitely planned to come right back and plug in. None of us even gave it a thought, until we got a call from B.J. from Germany; he told us John wasn't looking good, and that really hit us hard." – John Tierney

"John called me from Germany and we talked for over an hour. 'I hope this is the last treatment,' he said. 'I should be coming back soon.' Somehow, though, the topic came up about the unexpected: what if he didn't make it?"

"He said, 'Look, you and I have a handshake. You took us to the next level and if something were to

Our Journey: By B.J. Bohne

happen to me, I've talked to B.J. ... no matter what, our deal would always be honored.' It's like he knew there was a chance he might not make it."

– Daryl Lutes

B.J. was having dinner recently at the Trump Hotel in Chicago. Suddenly, as is the case every so often, an old friend broke out into an impromptu tribute to John Bohne.

"It wasn't only women who wanted to be with him, but guys too. Whether it was the famed Coach Ditka, the legendary Michael Jordan, or the powerful Mayor Daley, everyone wanted to hang out with John Bohne. Why? You couldn't put a finger it. All I can say is John Bohne was a man's man. Period." – B.J.

"A friend loveth at all times, And a brother is born for adversity."

Proverbs 17:17 (KJV)

The Bohnes.
Top row: Christiane Bohne Goesel, Edward Bohne, Arthur Bohne, Ainer Bohne, Fred Bohne, Lou Bohne Otter.
Bottom row: Meta Bohne Rush, Caroline Bohne, Christian Bohne, Edna Bohne, Dora Bohne

Grandpa Art Bohne and the twins (John and Jim)

L- R: Carol Bohne Wilson, John Bohne, Grandma Mary Bohne, Grandpa Art Bohne, Jane Bohne Byars and Jim Bohne

Rolling in his Cadillac. "Where does he think he is going?" O but he knew!

John & Gayle's wedding in Grandma Willadene's Rose Garden

Grandpa Ray and Grandma Willadene with Lance and B.J

"Mom practically raised us" - B.J

L-R: Gayle, John, Jonathan, Lance and B.J

The Bohne Family

John on safari in Botswana... Showing support for Mayor Daley's run for State's Attorney

ELECT DALEY

16th birthday in Paris with Dad

John with Mr. Entertainment himself, the legendary Wayne Newton

The Nicholas home in Grayslake

John's private aircraft

Pheasant hunting trip with Chicago Mayor Richard Daley

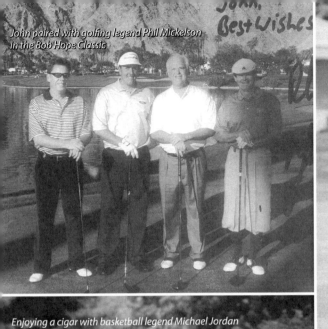
John paired with golfing legend Phil Mickelson in the Bob Hope Classic

B.J paired with Phil Mickelson a year later

Enjoying a cigar with basketball legend Michael Jordan

Jim Schmitz B.J's mentor with his infamous dog Yukon

John and B.J… just days before he passed away

The twins with their sisters: (L-R) John Bohne, Carol Bohne, Jane Bohne and Jim Bohne

At the SOS Family Village in Lockport

Imperial's A Team: L-R - Larry "Whitey" Gedmin, Dave Dobson, Rick Bohne, Lance, B.J, Darrel Lutes, Frank Tommanoff, Jay Mooncotch, Larry Eckardt, Bill Tierney

On a mission trip to Guatemala

Receiving the Spirit of Hope Award for our work with MDA

At the annual Citgo Golf Outing benefit for Muscular Dystrophy

IMPERIAL SERVICES, INC.
WORLDWIDE
Since 1969
1-888-HOIST IT

K SAFETY
SAFETY

B.J with Willadene

B.J with fiancé Irena

B.J with his trainer, Cory Probst and his executive assistant, Iva Boncheva

Daddy's girls, Kailey and Willadene

L-R: Jonathan Bohne, Gayle Bohne, B.J Bohne, Lance Bohne

Cranes - Its what we do. Its our passion!

Chapter Travel Tips

#22: Real Friends Don't Need To Keep Doing The Honeymoon Dance

Have you ever had a friend who acted as though they didn't know you simply because they hadn't seen you in a while? We all have them - high maintenance relationships that completely exhaust us. One defining characteristic of a true friend is that they don't make you have to re-qualify for access every time you are with them. It could be years since you last saw them, but it will feel as if it were yesterday. You should be able to pick up right where you left off. True friendships are not based on temporary emotions but, rather, on timeless commitment.

#23: Everyone Has An Opinion. Pick Your Circle of Counsel And Ignore The Rest

Someone said that opinions are like noses; everyone has one. I have seen more people fail to reach their potential because of people's unfavorable opinions. Where I come from in Africa, if you lose your reputation you are done, regardless of facts. In my tribe, people's opinions of you are very important. Unfortunately, you can't please everyone. Success sometimes demands that you do very unpopular things. It is thus prudent to pick a few people whose opinions matter to you, and listen to them; everyone else can keep piping away as you keep walking toward your destiny. John was a master at this.

Our Journey: By B.J. Bohne

#24 The Company You Keep Will Ultimately Influence Your Values

Take a good mango and put it in a bucket full of rotten ones. What will happen to it? It will rot. Now take a bad mango and place it in a bucket full of good ones; it will spoil the whole bucket-full of good mangoes. There are people who are in your life to stain, infect, mar, spoil or cause you to compromise your values. I call them Corruptors. Avoid them. All of us have fallen into the temptation of thinking we can somehow influence a friend to change. We also know what happens almost every time: the opposite. Like it or not, negative associations are contagious.

#25: True Friends Will Walk With You Even If It Is Inconvenient

Ever had a friend commit to getting old with you, only to turn on you, shut you out, and even attack you? I have. Sometimes, one of the ways you know someone is a true friend is by what they do when you are in trouble. Anyone can stay with you when you look good. Only a true friend will stay with you through both the bad and the good. They are not afraid to look bad because of their association with you. Here is what the Bible says, "A friend loves at all times . . ." (Proverbs 17:17 NIV)

#26: Only God Knows The Number Of Our Days

Having grown up under Idi Amin and other anarchic military regimes in my birth country of Uganda, I have seen a lot of death. I remember jumping over bodies of friends on my way to school. I have escaped many a killing raid and numerous mass bombings. I sometimes ask myself why I was spared. Perhaps you have wrestled with the same question

Imperial Crane

after the loss of a loved one. To this day, some of John's closest friends and family still wrestle with that question. Job declares, "Naked I came from my mother's womb, and naked I will depart. The LORD gave and the LORD has taken away; may the name of the LORD be praised." (Job 1:21 NIV) Everything we accumulate here ultimately remains here. The only thing we take with us is God's peace. So ask yourself this question: Have I been a good steward of my life?

When It Shouldn't Be Storming At All

If you see a glimmer in the rainstorm
Can it be that sunshine is there too?
If the hours are dark and gloomy
Can it be that light will soon come through?

When times are hard and needs are many
Do you know that someone prays for you?
When you feel lost and lonely
Do you know that someone cares for you?

O'er the world are hunger, desolations
Which some swear must always be –
But let us make the desolate fewer
And life better for all to see

Let's create a haven as far away as we can reach
For the lonely and the needy –
And with compassion encircle
So gently and with care
Every needy person who suffers everywhere

Let the comfort and the caring
Start with one right here.
With a prayer so strong and powerful
That each suffering needy person
Will sense that help is near

Our Journey: By B.J. Bohne

Let understanding and compassion
Begin right here with me
And pyramid the power of love
For all the world to see

Let care and concern for others
Over-run all barriers
And swept away like a torrent
All suffering and misunderstandings

Willadene
Take a Walk Upon a Rainbow and other
Poems and Prose
Copyright 1981

"For I am convinced that neither death nor life, neither angels nor demons, neither the present nor the future, nor any powers, neither height nor depth, nor anything else in all creation, will be able to separate us from the love of God that is in Christ Jesus our Lord."

Romans 8:38, 39 (NIV)

Chapter 7

John's Departure

"There is not a day that I look at his picture on my office desk, and not thank God for John Bohne. What a great man he was!"

– John Tierney

On October 8, 2003, John called Whitey from Germany. Whitey was pleasantly surprised to hear his voice, despite its noticeable weakness. After a short chat, John said to Whitey, "Hey, take care of Gayle."

Whitey was somewhat taken aback. "Why would he ask me to do this? And why me?" he wondered.

The following day, John Bohne passed away.

Dad Is Gone!

"When I heard the news, I walked to my desk and sat there in a daze, completely speechless. I couldn't be-

Our Journey: By B.J. Bohne

lieve it. One of my operators asked, 'John, are you al-
right?' 'No. I'm not okay. John just passed away!' The
operator lost it; broke down crying. I then walked into
John's office and took a long look at all his photos. He
loved to take pictures of memorable moments. As I
stared at the pictures, I recalled the rich history of ex-
periences we shared. I could remember the simple
things like how he would yell instructions at me from his
office. I remembered the old daily journal log - our bi-
ble, we called it – where we recorded jobs, hours and
operator's names long before everything became
electronic. Yes, a great man had just passed away." –
John Tierney

On that sad October morning, still rather stunned from the news, Bill Tierney called B.J. "B.J., I have terrible news for you. I got a call from Germany that your dad just passed away. I cannot believe this. I am very sorry." A deafening silence followed. He offered to call Gayle and his brothers and relay the news.

"No, I have to do that Bill," B.J. protested and hung up to call his mother.

"We were at the eighth hole at Butler National when
B.J. got a call from Bill. You could tell something was
wrong; he was visibly shocked as he echoed back
those chilling words to us: 'My dad just died!' He

Imperial Crane

turned to me after he hung up and asked, 'what do I do now, Ted?' 'Call your mother, B.J. She needs you right now.'" – Ted Alden, B.J.'s long time friend.

"Earlier that morning, Dad had called me. I would have never thought it might be the last time we would speak. For the most part, we had a nice conversation. In hindsight, I remember thinking he didn't sound like himself. Suddenly, he said, 'I gotta go. I'll speak to you later.' The next call was Bill Tierney telling me Dad was dead. I was shocked. I thought, 'How bizarre. He leaves to go out of town and I never see him again.'"
– Lance

B.J. called Gayle, then Jonathan.

"That call to Jonathan was probably one of the hardest phone calls I've had to make. For months, I had been telling them I thought Dad was going to be okay. When Jonathan broke down and demanded to know what had happened and how come he had died, I was speechless. It felt as though I had lied to him. Honestly, though, I really thought he was going to pull through." – B.J.

Gayle wasn't sure how Jonathan would take the news, with him being away in Arizona. John had tried to keep the severity of his illness from his youngest son. While both Lance

215

Our Journey: By B.J. Bohne

and B.J. had the opportunity to say their goodbyes – even though they really didn't know it at the time – Jonathan hadn't.

She feared the news would devastate her son. She called John's childhood friend, Greg Martin, who was at the University of Arizona in Tucson, and asked him to drive over to be with Jonathan; he did, and actually stayed with him until Jonathan had tied up his affairs with the school before traveling back to Chicago to mourn with the rest of the family.

Travel Tip:

Rarely Do We Appreciate Those Dear To Us Until It's Too Late

"I was on my way to college at Arizona State University when I got B.J.'s call that Dad was gone. I was upset, heartbroken and crushed. I cried hard. I could not understand. I really thought he was coming back home. I thought the treatments were working. I was confused.

Thankfully, Greg came to be with me. We flew home for the wake and funeral. It was horrible. I felt abandoned. I remember thinking, 'Well, I'll do whatever I want now. Who cares what happens to me? My authority figure is gone. There would be no one to set me straight or watch over me.' I really felt abandoned and alone." – Jonathan

Imperial Crane

Stunned

The news stunned everyone, particularly those who worked with John. No one, not even those who were aware of his illness, expected this.

"I didn't think John would die. He was telling me how great the clinic was, and how he would return home better." – Bill Tierney

"The clinic claimed that the treatment was successful, but there was an embolism. Of course, that raises the question that if it was such a fine clinic why wasn't it detected in time? I can still remember the last time I saw John in Munich. B.J. and I were getting ready to fly home the following morning and as he got into the limousine to go back to the treatment center, he hugged B.J. and cried. I looked at him and said, 'John you are coming back in one week.' It was then that I began to worry. Did he know something I didn't? I think that as hard as it was for us to see him go so suddenly, it was better for him to have gone this way. By every indication, we would have had to watch him deteriorate and see him suffer for months from the agonizing chemo. I only wish he could have lived longer. John had an astute business mind. He never beat about the bush; he shot straight. The sad thing is that in the last days of his life, he and I got real close.

Our Journey: By B.J. Bohne

Though we were sixty years old, it's as though we were kids again. He was my only brother, and I miss him." – Jim Bohne

"I had heard that he was doing okay. And then I got the phone call late in the night. John had passed. My mind flooded with memories. Here was a guy who was bigger than life; I mean, huge; a guy who had touched so many people; provided for so many families. And he was suddenly gone! What an honor to have been surrounded by such greatness! All I could think of were the good times we had together and all the accomplishments. In this industry, no one is there to toss you bouquets or pat you on the back. You are expected to perform, perform, perform! But, over the years, I came to look to John for that much needed affirmation and reassurance." – Ron Selby Jr.

Prior to his death, Lance had helped organize a sixtieth birthday bash for his father and Uncle Jim. John's mystic and pugnacious magnetism was infectious. Here was a guy who didn't go to college, but had the smarts and savvy of a Harvard MBA. When a family friend broke the news of his passing to Michael Jordan, he was visibly distraught.

He turned to the guys around him and said, "I don't think you guys understand, but the guy he is talking about – John Bohne – was a real life John Wayne!"

Imperial Crane

"I was at a friend's house when Jonathan called me. He kept repeating, 'Dad is dead. My dad is dead.' As I tried to come to terms with the news, desperation came over me. I felt as though I'd been punched in the stomach. My hope was gone, too. John was my key to the future; he was going to get me into the union. He was my hope and now that hope was gone. I felt scared. " – Fred Hunssinger

"I was at a refinery, managing our project there when the safety director, Herb Harmon, called me. 'John passed away!' The news hit me like a ton of bricks. I was so grateful that I had had that long conversation with him." - Daryl Lutes

"It was so sudden for everyone. Besides, he didn't broadcast it. I had just learned, the day before he died, that we had landed a big job to work on the Chicago White Sox U.S. Cellular Field in Brandenburg."

"I couldn't wait to tell him. The following day, I was traveling to Canada for my son's hockey tournament, and as we were sitting in line waiting to cross the border, I got the call from Whitey that he had passed away. He really left an impression on my life."

"Every now and again I ask, 'What would John do?'" – Rick Bohne

Our Journey: By B.J. Bohne

"B.J., I'm going with you," insisted Greg Martin.

"I'll be fine, Greg, you don't need to come," B.J. replied. He wanted to be alone for a while, maybe take some time to grieve. Having been his father's best friend for over thirty years, Greg would not take "no" for an answer.

B.J. was still in shock. The worst had happened and nothing could have prepared him for this. The great John Bohne dead? This was the man who had taught him so much about life. He had given him an identity and vision. Thoughts raced through his mind: "Who will help me? How am I going to work this out? Who is going to step up and manage everything and keep it all together?"

The long transatlantic flight to Germany was somber. Only a week before, he had made the same trip with measured optimism. But now, things were all jumbled inside his mind. He was confused, frustrated and sad.

B.J. and Greg rented a car at the Munich airport and made the scenic drive to Leonardo's Clinic in the wee hours of the morning. The head doctor, a silver-haired man around sixty years old, greeted them. He was overweight with slicked back, balding hair, and wore glasses; his thick German accent difficult to understand. He said, "Mr. Bohne was

Imperial Crane

progressing well with his treatment. The tumor on his liver was almost undetectable. But he developed complications from a lung embolism. A blood clot that started in his leg traveled through his body and lodged in his lungs. It prohibited his ability to breathe and that is what ultimately killed him."

Just like that. Wow!

> *"Although I found out later that this complication was not an uncommon side effect from cancer treatments, I could not help but think that perhaps if this had happened at a U.S. facility, they could have saved him. But, again, none of the major cancer treatment centers here would treat a sixty-year-old man with a history of heart disease and stage-three liver cancer." – B.J.*

Thanks to long time friends, the Schmaedekes, Schmaedeke Funeral Homes made immediate arrangements to fly John's body back with us to Chicago. Friends, family, and associates gathered in a moving tribute to his life.

> *"We had one of my operators drive a crane leading the long procession from John's house to the cemetery. Chicago Mayor Daley, dignitaries, clients, operators, agents, friends and family were all there. It was stately. You couldn't see a dry eye in the place." – John Tierney*

Our Journey: By B.J. Bohne

At the wake, Pastor Fred Bohne passionately talked about John's final days, and how, despite all his mistakes, faults and sins, John Bohne had sought forgiveness from God. He had committed his life into God's hands and was able to enjoy a rather peaceful end to his journey.

At the close of the memorial service, Pastor Fred invited all the mourners to invite Christ into their hearts. In a solemn prayer, almost everyone responded.

• • •

Travel Tip:

Regardless How Far Away We Fall, We Can Always Make Peace With God

"That service brought such closure for me. Knowing Dad made peace with God before he left this earth really comforted me, and still does to this day. It gives me a sense of peace. Sharing that moment with friends and family was priceless." – B.J.

• • •

After the funeral, Gayle invited everyone who could to follow the procession back to the house. "We talked all night about John, his life, and we shared the sweetest memories," recalls John Tierney.

"For the longest time after that, I would almost fall over whenever his brother Jim called the office. He sounds exactly like John."

Imperial Crane

What now?

A cloud of questions and uncertainty started to form around the company's future. What was going to happen to *Imperial Crane*? Could it really operate without John Bohne? Who would step up and take the reins of the business? John had worked so hard to gain respect in the entire industry; anyone who mattered knew him. His relationship equity was staggering.

> *"Dad left the company to all three of us. There was no stipulation as to who would do what. He didn't say B.J. was to be president. But seeing that I was already president of Imperial Crane Sales, it was natural that B.J. became president. He knew how to do the job, and in fact always had the potential to do it. We had to put the company before anything else. We had to put principles before personalities. There was no need for a power play or anything like that. Besides, I figured there was nothing to fight about. We just needed to work hard and keep this going." – Lance*

When word got out about the company's new leadership, fears and uncertainty concerning its future escalated from both within and outside the company. The perception was that the boys were not really interested in keeping the business. Out came the naysayers. "They're going to sell the company. They won't want to deal with all the banks, insur-

223

Our Journey: By B.J. Bohne

ance companies and contracts. What's to stop them from selling it and blowing all that money?"

> "Everyone kept speculating how everything was going to fall apart. We could see Imperial Crane's competitors positioning to take shots at our contracts. They knew that the guy who built the ship was out of the way. But they were wrong. B.J. stepped up. Lance stepped up big time too, and as a matter of fact, in my opinion, he was perhaps our best employee. The combination of Lance and B.J. wanting to keep this going ended those conversations." – Fred Hunssinger

> "Uncertainty quickly turned into fear for many. The obvious questions were in the air: "What are we going to do? Will the company continue?" Everything had run around John; he was Imperial Crane's president, CEO, and visionary. He **was** Imperial Crane. I remember going out to dinner with the family right after that and they started to talk about what was next. As the conversation proceeded, B.J. turned to me and said, 'Robert, don't worry about it. I will not sell the company. We are going to work hard. We will be okay.' That comforted me." – Robert Kaleta

Prior to his death, John had stipulated that B.J. would be the executor of his will. Attorney and columnist Joan Lisante painted the perfect picture of an executor's job in a 2003

Imperial Crane

Washington Post article. She said, "If you really want to know what executors do, go to a circus and watch the clown in the center of the ring juggle several balls while riding a unicycle."

Being the executor gave B.J. legal authority to make any decision on behalf of his father's estate; the first and most important being the decision of who would lead the company. In the interest of clarity and legal authentication, long-time friend and company corporate attorney Jack George of Daley & George, Ltd., fully endorsed B.J.'s appointment to president and CEO of *Imperial Crane Services*. It was not an issue of a power play; someone had to step up and make the critical decisions with regard to property, acquisition and liquidating of assets, and to the controlling of shares and all matters relating to their late father's estate. Thus, the responsibility fell squarely on B.J.

> *"When you become who I refer to as 'The Guy,' things are different. The buck stops with you. My heart went out to B.J., but I knew he would be fine."*
> *– Sam Palumbo*

As the dust slowly settled, in came the bills, including 2003 income taxes and the estate taxes, which the Internal Revenue Service was eager to collect. To ensure these items were handled properly, B.J. immediately engaged his corporate accountant Bob Hannigan, as well as an estate tax specialist

Our Journey: By B.J. Bohne

from one of Chicago's reputable accounting firms, Bansley and Kiener.

"First, I had to pay tens of thousands of dollars for detailed appraisals of the business and all of Dad's assets. When it was all said and done, we were hit with an enormous multi-million dollar estate tax. Without liquidating assets or selling off a bunch of cranes, I had no way to raise that kind of cash; so I turned to real estate. Dad had left his house in trust for Jonathan since, unlike Lance and I, he had no house at the time. So I could not touch that."

"Thankfully, there was a large building he had purchased for Prime Cable, later named the Comcast building, which had appreciated handsomely. Selling it would mean incurring a capital gains tax, but that was nothing compared to the 50 percent estate tax. I sold that off along with all his shares from Prairie Bank, a bank he actually co-owned at the time."

"The proceeds covered the entire amount owed to the IRS including his hefty income tax bill. I still remember writing that check; what relief! There were a lot of smaller, though critical, details regarding his estate that I had to close out, but I never let all that cripple me emotionally. I knew I had to deal with some of the consequences of Dad's decisions." – B.J.

Imperial Crane

Without really planning for it, John had bestowed a clean slate to his sons. What most people, including close friends, don't know, however, is that prior to his death John had been engaged in systematic estate planning for his family?

> *"For ten years, Dad had been gifting us percentages of the company. We had countless conversations regarding power transfers and so on. That taught me a lot. For the last ten years, I have had my mind wrapped around planning for my own estate. Though still in my early forties, I know it's never too early to think about it for the sake of my daughters and loved ones. Imperial Crane is worth a lot more than when Dad died. The last thing I want is for my loved ones to be hit with crippling taxes." – B.J.*

Although his death was sudden, John had performed adequate due diligence to ensure his loved ones would be taken care of in the unlikely event he had to leave this earth. I think we all have a lot to learn from John. One thing we cannot schedule is death. Whatever status, race or sex, all men and women die at some time; and often they die rather suddenly.

Gin

B.J. inherited the executive responsibilities of running *Imperial Crane*.

Our Journey: By B.J. Bohne

"John left the company to his boys, with B.J. in the driver's seat. He was the new boss, as Imperial Crane would remain a private family business. There were problems, though. First, both Lance and Jonathan were still struggling. Second, over the years I had seen how B.J. had been a source of frustration to John, all the way to the very end. In my opinion, he was in no shape or form to take over the company. I debated whether or not I would continue with Imperial Crane. The other problem was I was a partner with John. With him gone, I wasn't gonna take orders from his kids. To me, things didn't look good at all for Imperial Crane, except that the core components of the company held intact." – Jeff Bohne

Jeff did stay with Imperial Crane. For about a year after John's death, he didn't engage much with the day-to-day operational affairs of the company, but rather simply focused on doing his job, selling cranes, as he sat back and watched how things would pan out.

As B.J. scrambled to make sense of his next steps, he remembered one of his father's pastimes: gin. John was a consummate gin player. Gin is a two-player card game which uses the standard card deck. Players gain points by arranging cards into melds before their opponent can do the same. The winner must engage risk and intuition to knock the others off to "go gin".

Imperial Crane

John won every single gin tournament at Butler National. He was an aggressive, incisive player. Intuitive at recognizing what cards his opponents held, John had an extraordinary ability to anticipate his opponents' next move. Clearly, the game mirrored his life stance and personality.

Interestingly, B.J. only played one person in gin, ever: his father.

● ● ●

Travel Tip:

A Surefire Way Of Becoming the Best Is By Playing With the Best

"We would play for hours and he would crush me every time. For years, I never won a single game. One day, I had to fill in for him at a big black-tie gin tournament. I had never played anyone else and quite frankly had no idea how well I would do."

● ● ●

"That night I crushed everyone, winning over $9,000 in cash. I beat the best twenty gin players at Butler. It was pretty incredible. I mean, this is what these guys do, they play gin."

"Naturally, they wondered where I had learned to play. All I did was play my dad long enough to learn how to anticipate everyone else, and that was enough to win a major championship game." – B.J.

Our Journey: By B.J. Bohne

B.J. took those lessons and began to gain confidence. While he didn't really know how to make the big corporate decisions inherent to running a multi-million dollar company, he had been with his dad long enough to catch his cadence and language of leadership. In other words, after years of playing gin with an expert, B.J. was ready to play anything against anyone, for the best game of his life.

> *"As I wrestled through those first few months, so many alternatives presented themselves. Sure, we could have sold the company and moved on. I could just as easily have invited an investment group to come and take it over or do a joint venture with me. But all those alternatives meant one thing: loss of control; control, not so much financially, but philosophically and directionally. For one, those companies would only be interested in the bottom line. The rich family history and relationships that had been woven through the years would be meaningless to them. I thought about the Selbys, the Gedmins, the Tierneys, the Bohnes, and all the men and women with whom we had tirelessly worked to build this company. The decision was clear: we would push on to keep Imperial Crane going, no matter how difficult. Suddenly, it hit me: Imperial Crane was mine to make or break!" – B.J.*

Chapter Travel Tips

#27: Rarely Do We Appreciate Those Dear To Us Until It's Too Late

One of the most sobering realizations is the finality of death. It is on our deathbeds that we appreciate the shortness of our existence here on earth. Our wakes and funerals make for unspeakably painful experiences. "Why was I mean to him?" "Why did I not forgive her?" "I should have appreciated him more." "I wish I had told her how I felt." "I should have played with him more." Regrets that haunt us, long after those dear to us have left this earth. Here's a challenge: will you put this book down and draft that text or email, make a phone call, or turn to your dear ones and let them know how grateful you are for them?

#28: Regardless How Far Away We Fall, We Can Always Make Peace With God

The Bible says we have all sinned and have so desperately fallen short of God's standard. In fact, it says if we claim to be sinless, we make God a liar and deceive ourselves. That's right. We are all guilty, and for that, God's punishment is death. The good news is there is no such a thing as being too sinful for God. John 3:16 says God loved us so much that He sent His son to die for us. At the cross, Jesus took our punishment for sin. All He wants now is for us to recognize that we need Him, and to accept His precious gift of salvation.

Our Journey: By B.J. Bohne

#29: A Surefire Way Of Becoming The Best Is By Playing With The Best

Our mentors have the power to influence our success. In most African villages, this is the principle method of instruction for young men and women. For generations it has been the foolproof way of preserving traditions and values, and, until recently, transferring skills and knowledge. So, find a great player and play with them. Do this consistently, and you too will become great. Here is what the scriptures say, "He who walks with the wise shall be wise, but a companion of fools shall be destroyed." (Proverbs 13:20 NLT)

Take for Granted Nothing

Take for granted nothing
For too soon it may be gone.
The dewdrop only glistens
While it is shone upon.

The gentle breeze caresses
But too soon becomes a storm.
The rose unfolds to perfection
But with age loses its perfect form.

No city stands forever –
No man's a king for long.
So appreciate the gentle breeze
Before it comes too strong.

Willadene
A Child Can Dream and other Poems and Prose
Copyright 1981

A Train and a Jackrabbit   by Willadene

Part Three: The Legacy

"Do not be anxious about anything, but in every-thing, by prayer and petition, with thanksgiving, present your requests to God. And the peace of God, which transcends all understanding, will guard your hearts and your minds in Christ Jesus."

Ephesians 4:6, 7 (NIV)

Chapter 8

Our Company

"It's amazing what these kids have done with the business. To see where it is now compared to when we started is truly amazing."

– Larry Gedmin, a.k.a. Whitey

"Everyone was concerned about their jobs and the future of the company. As vice president, I needed to provide the confidence they craved. I assured them we would be continuing to do business; that it was not a matter of whether or not we would survive, but how we would move on after this tragedy." – Bill Tierney

Bill mapped out a move-forward plan for the first thirty days, by moving various personnel and their respective functions around. He had someone in mind to replace him, so he could step up and run the company. He set up a meeting with B.J. in order to lay out the plan. B.J. responded with five words that surprised Bill, words that would ultimately change the company: "I've got it under control."

Our Journey: By B.J. Bohne

"I knew he was competent, but I would have never imagined him stepping up that quickly and that decisively to take the reins and become president of Imperial Crane." – Bill Tierney

"Though the business was huge, I was always confident in B.J. I knew he was cut from the same mold as his father. And, like him, I knew he would take the necessary steps, and risks, to bring this company to even greater heights." – Robert Kaleta

"I gotta be honest; I was somewhat worried when he passed. What would happen to our arrangements? But this family has been incredibly generous to me. B.J. has been honorable to his father's commitments to me, and I will always respect him for that." – Daryl Lutes

Even with all of Jim Schmitz's coaching and his father's mentoring, B.J. still had many questions.

Without a doubt, he had big shoes to fill.

"Dad never taught me about insurance. That was his thing, there was always a piece he left only for himself to handle; he didn't believe in making himself completely irrelevant. After he passed, I was clamoring for answers to some of those functions he alone knew how to manage." – B.J.

Imperial Crane

In the USA, the average crane rental company carries roughly $5 million in insurance every year. In comparison, Imperial Crane carries over $50 million of coverage, so it's a very important part of their due diligence.

> *"Our insurance agent, assuming we weren't going anywhere, especially at a time like that, neglected to respond to my questions despite repeated inquiries. It looked like he didn't care. Out of frustration, I fired him. Sure it cost us some money, but I felt I needed to make a bold statement regarding the courtesy of a callback and, I didn't want anyone to take our business for granted. Well, that got his attention. Eventually, he worked his way back in, and a year later, he won our contract back. To this day, we enjoy an immensely fruitful working relationship. His company has done a great job for us." – B.J.*

My Inheritance

Prior to his death, John had begun sensing an impending shift in the crane business. He had been there before. His belief was that for Imperial Crane to position itself effectively, they had to expand; buy more cranes.

That is exactly what he did, he bought millions of dollars worth of new cranes. As a result, with John's sudden death,

Our Journey: By B.J. Bohne

Imperial Crane was left with over $15 million in corporate debt.

"In addition to all the executive decisions that came with his new position, B.J. inherited another problem: financial institutions. We had around ten banks that needed assurance there would be someone to lead this company successfully and to make doubly sure our debt was serviced. With John gone, they were not confident in our future capabilities and, frankly, they started to panic." – Bill Tierney

• • •

Travel Tip:

The Best Person You Can Be Is You

B.J. remembers meeting with bank executives in his father's office, along with senior staff and his mother, Gayle.

• • •

"Here I was at the head of this massive company. I remembered how brutally the banks had dealt with our friend Pat Walsh. I thought, 'Man, if the banks are coming after Pat like that, they are surely coming for me.' We had way more debt and so much more to lose. As I tried to wrap my head around the future, I could remember Dad's leadership style, his methodology and how he ran the business by intimidation. When he entered the room, everyone stopped. I, for one, have a totally different approach; I don't want fear to

Imperial Crane

be the first thing my employees feel when they see me. Sure, they know I am their boss, but I work extra hard to make them feel safe and comfortable around me. Instead of focusing on making sure everything runs like I want, I prefer to celebrate strengths and build bridges. As for our clients, I prefer wining and dining them, instead of holding them to their commitments. It's these differences that I had to consider as I worked to forge new relationships with our lenders."
– B.J.

Was he tempted to lay down a heavy hand especially when some of his major clients seemed to take advantage of his leniency and transparency? Sure, but he couldn't. No matter how hard he tried, he could not be John Bohne. Thus, he made a pivotal decision: "Since I cannot be my old man no matter how hard I try, I think its best I be B.J."

The Banks

"We were very worried about the company. Would B.J. step up? Was he even able to? Frankly, with his lifestyle, I wasn't sure. But boy, did he ever turn around drastically and quickly. When he looked at the numbers those first couple of days and learned how much debt we needed to service, he was taken aback, even though he didn't show it. A week after John passed away, he got alone with Bill and I and announced, 'Look guys, I am not doing anything differ-

Our Journey: By B.J. Bohne

ent with this company. As far as I am concerned, it's running just the way Dad wanted it to. Now, unless something drastic happens or goes really wrong, things will go on exactly as they have been going. Nothing is going to change that.' That gave us a lot of comfort and confidence. He treated us royally, as his dad had. He really won us over. We don't own this company, but we would do anything for Imperial Crane." – John Tierney

For a while, Imperial Crane kept its operation intact, even as the new leadership continued to win the trust of its clients and the industry at large.

It was in early 2005 and the boys were struggling to keep all the pieces flowing smoothly together. They had just acquired a smaller crane company up north and Lance suggested they hire a consulting firm to help clarify the delineation of roles and streamline the overall direction of the company.

"Dad was such a control freak. He ran a $30 million dollar company without controllers or financial officers. I couldn't do that, given my limited experience. So yes, it was a great suggestion by Lance to get this kind of input. Initially, though, I was reluctant. We have a great accounting firm. Why pay some guy a hundred and some thousand dollars to tell me what I already

Imperial Crane

know?' But it's been great. I don't think I could have accomplished as much without someone like Dave." – B.J.

For several months, Dave Dobson and his team performed several diagnostic assessments of the company.

> *"John was a very influential figure throughout the entire crane industry. He was a towering personality. He handled all the contracts, insurance, payroll, everything! He was Imperial Crane. So after he passed there was an immediate void. With the various moving parts – equipment, staff, even real estate – there was a critical need to restructure the company if they were to remain competitive and profitable." – Dave Dobson, Chief Financial Officer, Imperial Crane Services.*

Dave's team identified two areas of need: Imperial Crane needed a controller and a human resources manager. With Lance and B.J.'s blessing, they brought in several candidates without much success.

> *"After futilely trying to fill the position, my boss encouraged me to throw in my hat. B.J. was happy with the proposition and I was hired. Initially, I came in as a controller, but as we grew, I became CFO, and shortly afterward, I hired a controller to work under me. We immediately embarked on an aggressive campaign*

Our Journey: By B.J. Bohne

The company had two main banks, MB Financial and Hinsdale Bank, along with a multitude of smaller ones.

Meanwhile, an economic recession was looming. Major banks, insurance corporations, mortgage companies and construction conglomerates began to crumble. Economists called it an economic downturn.

"Naturally, I feared the worst. Imperial Crane held loans with fourteen banks." B.J. recalls, "Just then, I got a call from one of our lenders, 'Mr. Bohne, we need you to come pay off your entire loan.'"

"You are kidding, right?" he replied in shock. He was thinking, "Great. As if I don't have enough on my plate." "What's the problem? Imperial Crane has never missed a payment with you," B.J. continued. "All my cranes are out there working. You know I can't pay off the entire loan."

"Well, we need to sell or consolidate, but whatever you do, you must settle up; we have to unload all our assets to other banks." B.J. would learn that three of the fourteen banks that held his loans were going out of business. "Selling

Imperial Crane

was not an option for me," says B.J., "We would get murdered on the pricing."

He started looking for new financing, but banks were squeamish. They weren't interested in lending. The housing boom was over and no one wanted to touch anything to do with construction.

•   •   •

Over the next few months, Imperial Crane would sell a couple of cranes and bundle and refinance some of the smaller loans with the more stable lenders.

"It looked as though we had dodged that bullet, thanks to some creative juggling with my team. But as I was trying to breathe from the stress of it all, my main bank, MB Financial, called. They held over $10 million of our total debt load and they were worried. The principle – Dad – the man they had really lent the money to wasn't there to guarantee the on-going success of the business. Besides, they too were beginning to feel the stress taking place across the entire banking sector. They told me they were not confident in our future. Although we were making our payments, our margins were miserable and

Our Journey: By B.J. Bohne

they knew it. So they imposed new restrictions on us. They wanted to see our daily cash-flow reports: receivables, payables, and so on."– B.J.

This circus, as B.J. calls it, cost Imperial Crane well over a million dollars in consultancy and auditor's fees.

> *"This was a very stressful period for me, but more so for our team, which at the time totaled over two hundred crane operators and fifty office staff. These dedicated men and women had mortgages to pay and families to support. A collapse of our company would affect thousands of people. They deserved my commitment and protection. We had to make this work, regardless." – B.J.*

Eventually, B.J. persuaded the banks that Imperial Crane was fiscally fit, and that they would continue doing business profitably. He assured them that they would cap their growth by holding off on any major expansion and subsequent crane purchases, and focus on effectively reducing their debt.

They held true to that commitment for the next couple of years and soon the banks began to warm up to them and, in fact, wanted to double their lines of credit. As his dad would have done, B.J. took that money and bought more cranes, effectively doubling their fleet and maxing out their credit lines to almost $90 million.

> *"As the banking sector continued to get stressed, banks would change officers and account managers in order to stay on top of their clients. Consequently, every time I applied for credit line increases or attempted to restructure our loans, I had to remake our case with new loan officers who carried new fears. It was a headache."– B.J.*

This was a time when the company could have chosen to be safe; to pace itself and not risk too much, given the economic environment and internal company dynamics. They didn't. B.J.'s gut was telling him to grow and risk even more.

> *"After John died, B.J. took the reins of the company and instead of pulling back or treading softly, as many would have expected, he chose to grow–very aggressively! Personally, my role expanded to include operations management. We expanded into new territories, locations and satellite offices. For a year, I worked as Project Manager for a refinery project, managing a fleet in excess of one hundred cranes and two hundred and fifty employees. After that, I returned back to Bridgeview where I was appointed Vice President of Operations. Today, I oversee the daily organization*

Our Journey: By B.J. Bohne

and function of the company in all of our locations. At the time of this writing, I am dispatched to the Conoco Phillips Refinery in Borger, Texas, where we are completing a major turnaround project with a large equipment fleet and nearly one hundred and fifty employees." – Larry Eckardt

B.J. believes that successful businessmen, such as his dad, feel the pulse of their industry. For them, business is more than mere numbers and graphs; it's more than counting beans.

Every company, especially banks, has bean counters; those people who spend their days crunching numbers and assessing risk. They create opposing scenarios and play fictitious economic trajectories to no end.

If there is one group of people B.J. had a problem with during the first few years after his father passed, it was - and continues to be - the bean counters. He had the agonizing task of persuading them that the company would continue to enjoy success despite the odds.

"By the time a bank's bean counter has enough information to chart projections, its old information. The trend or cycle has already turned. Why? Because the numbers or records from which they project future performance is taken from previous performance. In reality, it is outdated before they begin." – B.J.

Imperial Crane

While Imperial Crane was haggling and wrestling with its lenders, a massive economic downturn, fueled by a housing crisis, was encroaching.

> *"In 2005, Florida was booming. I seized what I thought was an opportunity with elevators. We literally had every high-rise in Florida, and had at least thirty-six elevators operating. Just as we were about to make money, the housing market crashed and we got bruised." – Jeff Bohne*

Behind the crash were some of the largest lenders in the world. B.J. could understand the complexities in a completely new light, given his own odious experience.

> *"Relegating the housing disaster to mere greed, as many have, is irresponsible and shortsighted. I really believe that if the government's bean counters had worked with folks to help them stay in their homes right away, not years later, we would have averted this disaster. To me, it reiterates how out of touch bean counters can be. Financial institutions, even governments, are not always right. In fact, they are often wrong and some of them are completely out of touch. Just because they have accountants and statisticians with school smarts doesn't mean they always know what they are doing." – B.J.*

Our Journey: By B.J. Bohne

Stepping Out

Shortly thereafter, a large refinery approached Imperial Crane with a game-changing proposition. A competing crane company with the exclusive contract to service their plant had two major accidents, one of which resulted in $200 million in damages. They were desperate.

Imperial Crane had rented a few cranes to them over the years and they had become familiar with the company's unmatched safety standards.

> *"I remember it like it was yesterday. Here I was negotiating one of the biggest contracts in my life. This was the big-league. Across the table was one of the largest corporations in the world. So we danced."*

> *"When they said 'jump', we jumped. For over twelve months, we went back and forth, spending hundreds of hours going through excruciating details with a fine-toothed comb. Finally, we were happy and they were happy." – B.J.*

However, there was a catch. In order for them to comfortably sign off on the deal, Imperial Crane had to ensure they had the capacity to service and, more importantly, to maintain, their biggest customer and long time supporter, *Citgo Refinery* in Lamont.

Imperial Crane

The problem was that their fleet was not large enough; they had to buy more cranes. In a daring move, B.J. ordered over $50 million worth of new cranes. That one order would effectively double the size of their fleet.

> *"That was a crazy decision since, even though the market was slowly beginning to recover, we didn't have the contract yet. But without the cranes, we could not comfortably service the contract. Everyone was freaking out. The numbers were scary. I could have simply walked away and played it safe but I didn't, because somehow inside my gut, I knew this was the right move to make." – B.J.*

Imperial Crane won the contract and promptly ordered the cranes. As they began to arrive, the deal suffered delays and stalled for six punishingly long months. Then, the company started paying through the nose for the cranes as, one by one; they sat on the lot waiting for the job to begin.

> *"Looking at those cranes gave me a stomach ache. I started to panic. Aside from the fact that they had negotiated our profit margins to a mere sliver, the economy was beginning to spiral. I knew their bean counters were aware of how much the cranes cost me, and what the profit margins on each crane would be. But did they really care? I am not begrudging*

Our Journey: By B.J. Bohne

them here; in their defense, it was a tight cash flow situation." – B.J.

Eventually, the job began and the cranes got to work. It would be another twelve months before the job started to realize some revenue and Imperial Crane began to see some light at the end of the tunnel.

● ● ●

Travel Tip:

Sometimes Life Will Challenge You to Take a Risk That Will Either Sink or Launch You

It looked as though the plan was working.

"Those were tough times. But we got to see some of our principles at work. That deal was a result of our diligence at the refinery when we only had a handful of cranes." They didn't merely call us out of the blue. I have always told my guys that no job is inconsequential."

● ● ●

"We are to take every customer seriously. We must return all calls and treat every client with respect, because you never know if that guy will return again or, more importantly, if he or she will refer us to the next game-changing deal." – Bill Tierney

Imperial Crane

"Recapture Deflation?"

One day, Imperial Crane got a call from the same refinery; they wanted to have a meeting. The room was filled with over five hundred vendors. They announced: "Hey, you guys know what's going on out there. The economy is crumbling, and everyone is tightening up."

"There is a recession and we want to capitalize on this depressed market and recapture the deflation in the market place. We want all of our vendors to give us a twenty-five percent price reduction."

In addition, they wanted to reinstate Imperial Crane's responsibility for a property tax that they had earlier agreed to assume. And then came the clincher, "We need this done, or we are going to look for someone else."

B.J. was stunned. He felt completely blindsided.

"I grew up on integrity and honor in business. Quite frankly, I don't need a piece of paper. We can shake on any deal and I will stand by it. This is how I was raised. It's how my old man did business. So for me this was shocking and foreign, particularly after dancing around for a year, working through details, crossing T's and dotting I's. What did we do all that for? How do we redo a three year contract just like that, never

257

Our Journey: By B.J. Bohne

mind the small print? If all that work can be terminated within thirty days, then why waste the time? I was bewildered. – B.J.

Had Imperial Crane's attorneys missed something? No, they hadn't. Was the refinery violating a contract or doing anything illegal? No, they weren't. What they wanted to do was completely within their rights because the contract allowed for these maneuvers in the fine print. The bottom line was they were the big boys – one of the largest corporations in the world. Compared to them, Imperial Crane was a tiny dab in their arsenal. And with the economy tanking, Imperial Crane was at a disadvantage. "I discovered firsthand what it's like to be a regional company negotiating with a global billion dollar behemoth," B.J. recalls. "If anyone is to cave in, it is the smaller player."

Travel Tip:

Without Integrity, Business Arrangements Mean Little or Nothing

"I longed to talk to my old man. What would he do? How would he handle this one? I think I know what he would have done: he would have told the men to pack the cranes up and head out. Would they have come after him legally? Not likely, as we had all the

Imperial Crane

cranes; they needed us. Regardless, knowing the old man, he would have told them where to go and walked away from the table. Remember, he threatened to walk away from the table when he only had a handful of cranes. Make no mistake: my old man was a dictator. And I say that admiringly. He had the courage to stand up to anyone, even when the consequences were severe. It's at times like that I sure wish I had more of him in me. I am a diplomat. Both personality traits have their merits and demerits. Here is one important thing: when Dad made a deal, you could take it to the bank, come rain or shine. He was going to do anything to hold up his end. It's what he taught me and I lived by it. When I commit to something or someone, it doesn't matter how hard it hurts afterward. We have a deal, and I will honor it. So here I was looking at a signed contract with a major corporation that was not worth the paper it was written on. I am not John Bohne, though; he would have taken that gamble. Maybe that is a weakness I have. That was one of those times I sure wished he was right there with me." – B.J.

Technically, they were well within their rights to make any changes to the agreement, because every such contract has an out or an escape tacked at the back page of some ending section somewhere, allowing for the alteration of terms. Any contract is only a temporary framework of under-

259

Our Journey: By B.J. Bohne

standing. And in this case, the bigger player always holds the power. B.J. quickly figured that out and instead of crying about it, he knew they had to gather themselves and get back to the negotiating table. Other companies were on Imperial Crane's heels for their big contract. Everyone was hurting and desperation was rampant, especially in the construction industry.

> *"The new refinery's proposal put us in a real dilemma. While other contractors had margins to negotiate, we didn't. Besides, they didn't have to pre-order $50 million worth of materials. We had razor-thin profit margins and any changes would effectively erase them. We tried to negotiate, 'You guys know we are making nothing off this deal to begin with? You know we are in a squeeze here?' They didn't care. They were the only game in town and with the construction market in the tank, other companies were beginning to line up, offering sweetheart deals to replace us. I knew we had to close on these negotiations fast. I had extended the company to make this work. We had hit a crisis which could potentially sink our ship. And to make matters worse, all our eggs were in one basket." – B.J.*

Thus, they began the exasperating negotiations. Six months later, they settled on a 5 percent concession, which further deteriorated their already low profit margins.

Imperial Crane

Bailouts

For the following few months, B.J. had to get back to his banks and renegotiate new terms with them.

"As my banks struggled with their bad debts, primarily in the housing market, they looked for ways to boost their profitability. That meant targeting their successful accounts to increase fees or consolidate losses. Despite the slowing construction industry, Imperial Crane was a solid company with a strong equity position. Instead of sticking our heads in the sand and wishing for things to get better, I decided to take a more aggressive position. I was convinced that the market provided a great opportunity to buy new and used equipment. However, our lenders didn't agree with this. Consequently, we spent over $1 million on consulting firms so we could generate reports illustrating our claims." – B.J.

"Cars for Clunkers? Too Big to Fail? These concepts are ridiculous. Where were the Cranes for Clunkers programs to help all the crane manufacturers and crane dealers? Unlike the auto industry, we did not rely on anyone. Companies in our industry tightened their belts, cut costs, and did what they had to do in order to survive; and some didn't. I don't think it was a great idea to bail out the banks. We now know that most of

Our Journey: By B.J. Bohne

them used that cash to shore up their balance sheets, instead of using it to increase loans to consumers. The bailout also made it much more difficult to negotiate with them, since they had become newly empowered by the government."

"Sure, this government intervention may have saved some overextended banks, but I believe other more disciplined banks would have stepped in and bought the failing bank assets at pennies on the dollar. This resulting free market dynamic would have encouraged the remaining banks to negotiate better terms with their customers. I believe that, in the long term, this simple action would have saved us from the lingering recession, which some experts believe is still on-going at the time of this writing. If the government had to be involved, which I object to, they should have made loans available to businesses directly, thus enabling companies to purchase products, in my case, cranes, which would inevitably result in job creation. Let's talk about another example of governmental intervention: General Motors."

"Sure, the government bailed them out, but is the company any better off today? They can't even hire good executives and managers because high-caliber executives are often squeamish about working for the government. So, it would be good for the government

to sell its shares and get out, right? Well, not so simple. If the government sold its shares today, the taxpayers would lose $17 billion. Where is the success? A million jobs saved? Really?"

"If they had not been bailed out, I guarantee you other car manufacturers would have bought their assets and kept their skilled employees (as has been the case in similar situations in other parts of the world). Many companies go through structured bankruptcies, which means not everyone gets fired. I am willing to bet that had the government not interfered, GM would have re-emerged a leaner, more productive and profitable company." – B.J.

Coping

Did B.J. have doubts about his success? You bet he did, but he didn't dwell there; he couldn't afford to. "This was no time for pity parties," he said, "I had to keep going, no matter how grim I felt inside. I didn't always want to go to the office. But I'd say to myself, 'B.J., you get up and make this work.' My days were filled with executive meetings with staff and with our lenders. As you can imagine, that wasn't always fun."

To cope with the pressure, B.J. did and still does several things:

Our Journey: By B.J. Bohne

First, he drew closer to God.

I remember when an old friend, Rickey Crawford, asked if one of his friends, a successful businessman, could join us on a missions trip to Guatemala. Naturally, I needed to know more about this guy who wanted to come to a third world country with an African evangelist. We had a great time, which really impacted his life. I was impressed by the fact he recognized that nothing in this world could generate the buoyancy he needed to weather the storms raging around him. Like his father, he had recognized his deep need for God in his life.

He has since committed to giving care to his spiritual life. That doesn't mean he is perfect or without fault. It means he relies on the grace of God to carry him through the ups and downs of life.

> "After my dad died, I learned to turn to God as my Father. Faced with all these challenges and personalities, I had to lean on Him for comfort, for clarity, for peace. Spending time with God both privately and at our Church replenished my soul. That's how Dr. Dennis and I became close."

> "Allowing God's Word to permeate my mind helps me keep my priorities straight. I know that without Him, I can do nothing. Recognizing that gives me great

Imperial Crane

peace and confidence. In fact, the only time I struggle today is when I try to handle everything myself." – B.J.

Second, B.J. decided to get serious about his health.

Almost every single day, B.J.'s trainer, Cory Probst, drives over to his house and for at least two hours, he works diligently to keep his body in shape.

> *"Why do I have to work with Cory, my trainer, every morning for two grueling hours? Is it because it's fun? Do I enjoy being screamed at, or feeling my muscles literally burn as I get pushed to the limits of my physical endurance? No sir. It's because I want to be energetic and healthy. I want to be strong and to live a long, fulfilling life. The discipline helps me remain focused. It helps me get set for the challenging day ahead."* – B.J.

> *"It was Lance who introduced me to his brother, B.J. He wasn't looking for a trainer at the time; he had his own regiment."But one workout session changed it all. He had realized how hard it was to keep self-motivated, and needed someone to scream in his ear to keep lifting, keep eating well, in order to stay physically fit. He hired me right away and I have trained him ever since. Today I work out with the guy daily,*

Our Journey: By B.J. Bohne

and we have become friends. I treasure our friendship and on many occasions, he has been a role model and father figure to me. I am impressed by his sense of balance, his work ethic, and his passion for his family. For someone in his position, it's really hard to know who is hanging out with you because of you, or because of what you have. B.J. seems to be able to see through the mist." – Cory Probst

Third, he got back to golfing.

That might not sound important to many of us, but to B.J., golf is more than a game. It's a getaway which carries with it great memories and immense rejuvenation.

John and B.J. did a lot of golfing together; winning numerous trophies at renowned clubs such as Big Foot Country Club, Midlothian Country Club and Butler National Golf Club.

"I was with him when he had a hole-in-one on the fifth hole at Butler National; he was with me on the eighth hole when I had a hole-in-one; I was with him when he had a hole-in-one at Bass Lake Country Club in Wisconsin. I still remember when we won, hands down, the one hundred-year-old Father-Son tournament, the Pater Filius Tournament at Midlothian Country Club, after unsuccessfully trying for over twenty years. This is the oldest Father-Son tournament in the country."

Imperial Crane

"We had many moments together having hole-in-one contests. Actually, I recently made my seventh hole-in-one, beating Dad's record of four. I can say that it is while golfing that I discovered this cool dad I never knew I had." – B.J.

• • •

Travel Tip:

**To Grow
With Balance,
You Must
Give Attention
To Your
Body, Soul
and Spirit**

• • •

"For years, Dad played in the famed Bob Hope Classic in Palm Springs. The last year he played was 2003, just prior to his death. That year, he was paired with golfing legend Phil Mickelson, indisputably one of the greatest players ever. It was real special to me that after Dad passed, I was invited to play in his spot the following year. Phil Mickelson was there too, and, being the top player in the tournament, everyone wanted to partner with him. It was a pleasant surprise when I won the blind draw to be his partner! That Saturday, as we played together, he reminisced about playing with Dad, our business and Arizona State University, where he also attended." – B.J.

B.J. remembers John solving the biggest problems while golfing. Today, he uses it to reflect and to imagine what his father would do if he were here.

Our Journey: By B.J. Bohne

"Although all the women in my life have had problems with me playing golf, the game gives me a way to de-stress. I can still hear my daughter Kailey lamenting, 'You're going golfing again?' This morning, my three-year-old, Willadene, asked me where I was going, and when I said "golf", she had the exact same response – "again?"

"Whether they eventually take up the game seriously or not, I am trying to get them interested in it. I only want them there so we can spend some time together, as it's a big part of my life." – B.J.

Consolidation

B.J.'s first focus was the loans. Even with his dismal profit margins, he kept a diligent hand on his payments, reducing his debt load. In other words, by servicing his debt, he was building equity in his cranes. In a relatively short time, Imperial Crane was sitting on more than $20 million in equity.

"Our primary bank had internal structural changes that affected us. With every change in personnel, we had a new rep that needed to be educated. In addition, like most banks, they were inflexible. Earlier, I had tried to get a bigger line of credit, but it was like pulling teeth. The other problem was that we were also using term debt. We needed to transition to an asset-

Imperial Crane

based scenario, which would afford a company like ours the needed flexibility to raise and lower our debt structure predicated on the ebb and flow of our business. It was time to shop around!" - Dave Dobson

B.J. wanted to find one bank to take care of his entire debt. He was weary of the constant stress tests. Clearly, his current lenders doubted the company's ability to keep its payments and service its debt. Because all the loans had to be personally guaranteed by B.J., his credit score plummeted from all of the constant credit inquiries.

"Whenever we needed additional funding, I would go out and shop the market. Consequently, we had fourteen fragmented creditor arrangements, with no intercreditor relationship. This meant if one creditor decided to pull out, I had to go scrambling to replace them in order to avoid a potential forced sale of the collateralized equipment. This was good as long as everyone was playing ball with us, but if one of them went belly up or bailed for any reason, everything would collapse like a house of cards." - Dave Dobson

B.J. initiated closed door negotiations with two major lenders: GE Capital, a huge global lender, and BMO Harris, a solid North American bank. His principal aim was to find a lender – one lender – that would carry his entire $65 million debt. And to his pleasant surprise, both lenders were willing

Our Journey: By B.J. Bohne

to work with him. Although he was impressed by GE Capital's package, he was not comfortable with their size. Aside from the fact they had to outsource Imperial Crane's banking needs (they are not a bank), his dealings with large multinationals had taught him a thing or two about big corporations.

> *"Because I am a personable guy, I wanted more than a mere credit line. I wanted a relationship with our lender. When I compared both packages, I wondered how personal I could get with a bank that financed giant airline companies and small countries. I could imagine that if we ever had a major issue, they would simply demand a sell-off of my cranes." – B.J.*

I like how Dave Dobson put it. He said, "If we stubbed our toe, they'd be all over us, and our iron would go pretty quick!" Initially, they tried to partner the two lenders, with GE Capital providing the capital and BMO Harris servicing their banking needs. As those conversations ensued, it was clear BMO Harris had a significantly more flexible customer relations model than GE Capital. Says Dave, "We needed someone who could sit down at the table with us and at least have a listening ear to our issues."

In November 2011, Imperial Crane refinanced its entire loan portfolio, and what a difference that made.

Imperial Crane

One loan with one stable bank – BMO Harris.

"For years we were undercapitalized. As a rule, lenders don't look ahead; they look back in order to make their decisions, but we had to persuade them to take some risk with us. We had to convince them to view our relationship as more of a partnership, which most banks don't even understand. Typically, they are the lender and the customer is the borrower, period. Consequently, we were able to put together an agreement with BMO Harris that consolidated all the debt, including all the receivables. Today, we have a hybrid arrangement of term and asset-based structure that works very well for us. Instead of having fourteen different arrangements with fourteen different lenders, we have one arrangement with BMO Harris. Our financial package, although much more sophisticated with mechanisms requiring critical monthly attention, affords us a lower cost of funds or fixed interest rate for a lower term, which has saved us a lot of money. In looking back at the current success we enjoy, we needed to do this. " – Dave Dobson

By the time the deal closed, B.J. had reduced his debt by $10 million, so he had a comfortable cushion. In addition, he reduced their interest payments by $100,000 a month.

Our Journey: By B.J. Bohne

The added bonus, for the first time in the company's history, ensured its debt would be secured by its assets and the company would be able to stand on its own merits.

> *"I believed that, finally, the bean counters saw our true value. Although I would like to think of myself as endowed with a good measure of brilliance and courageous foresight, I know the opposite is true. If I had the choice, I would have elected to remain with our fourteen banks; I would have chosen to remain safe. What looks like a brilliant business move is something that was forced upon us. Today, we are in good shape. Imperial Crane has a structured deal, which allows the company to purchase approximately $7 million in new cranes each year, while paying down our debt by $3 million. We are in the strongest position we have ever been in the history of the company. All I needed to do was roll with it. The one thing I did was something that Dad taught me - I made a decision. Dad always knew how to make a decision."* – B.J.

As B.J. pondered the lessons of the season, he knew that the company had dodged a big bullet. Did he get everything he wanted? No, but today Imperial Crane has tripled the size of its fleet, and can now easily bid on the largest jobs in the country. By every estimation, the company is a much bigger player because of those hard decisions.

Imperial Crane

"B.J. has always been a big-picture guy and a great executioner. Whenever I needed something, he got it done. He definitely took after his dad who always thought out of the box and saw opportunities long before anyone else did. I am not surprised at how well he has done." – Pat Walsh

Moving Our Eggs

After Imperial Crane had resolved the deflationary issue, the refinery became enthralled in a larger disaster. Everyone, including the U.S government, was after them.

Further cuts were announced, as they had to move resources to deal with the gigantic financial implications.

"We have too many of our eggs in one basket. We need to branch out," B.J. announced to his team.

"What? Now? We are in the middle of a recession. No one is lending any money. This is not the time for any risky moves," his team echoed back.

They were both right. Granted, the financial climate was less than favorable for any vociferous business maneuvering; the company was too invested in this one large contract. His proposition was completely counter-intuitive.

Our Journey: By B.J. Bohne

"I got my sales team together and gave them a new mandate: expand. We have new cranes here, so you guys go get new accounts. Our refinery deal is great, but it's not going to be here forever."

"I don't want to have all our eggs in one basket. The team brought in new contracts and at the time of this writing, we've closed on a three-year deal with one of the largest companies in the country."

• • •

Travel Tip:

Don't Put All Your Eggs In One Basket

"Once again, I leveraged our positives and gains for our greater good, and, by God's grace, we came through. Has it been smooth even after that? Not at all. They have short-paid us, late-paid us, asked for extended remittance terms, and so on. But we keep moving forward." – B.J.

• • •

Today, Imperial Crane continues to outperform all previous expectations. As of this writing, they have quadrupled the fleet of a few cranes to a fleet of hundreds, not including the couple hundred they rent from competitors all over the country. In addition, they have also quadrupled the revenues to over $100 million annually, while continuing to reduce their debt.

Imperial Crane

"Today, we are a financially sound company, well able to meet all our bank covenants. Our balance sheet looks great. Our bottom line is solid. Our financial reporting has been upgraded and from an operations perspective, our entire system has been streamlined; our vendor relationships are better because of available cash flow; if B.J. wants to buy a new crane today, it's no longer a scramble. We get it done fast! We are paying down our debt and growing stronger every day. Are we there yet? No. Our costs are rising. For example, we have a Cadillac health insurance program controlled by the union. Each year, costs keep rising, especially as we get closer to the implementation of the health care bill."

"At the end of the day, we must make a profit in order to exist. So our pricing has to go up in order to stay in business. The fees built into the new healthcare law are going to trigger additional costs, which we don't have currently. The tax cuts expiring at the end of the year will also result in significant costs to us. Without some relief, our profitability will diminish unless we raise our prices or reduce expenses. For any company like ours, the biggest expense is payroll. So we either pay people less or have fewer jobs. Ultimately, it will affect jobs!"

- Dave Dobson

Our Journey: By B.J. Bohne

"I think everything has worked out really well," says Lance, "Thank God everyone else has stepped up to the plate to create this success. I am so glad to see how well we are doing."

> "Why is Imperial Crane successful? Simple: The grace of God, a lot of luck, and lots of guts! This company was founded by John Bohne, whose early success can be directly attributed to bold, aggressive, and fearless decision making. He started with one crane, one employee, and built an empire. John surrounded himself with the right people, and their efforts and dedication to the company have fostered its remarkable growth and success. He instilled this same ideology into his sons, and so the company has continued with that vision. Imperial Crane has experienced incredible expansion and growth since B.J. has taken over, despite a poor economy and lackluster financial environment." – Larry Eckardt

Chapter Travel Tips

#30: The Best Person You Can Be Is You

God is not random or haphazard. He is precise and deliberate. Even before the universe was created, He had a plan for you. You and I are not here by accident or mistake. Each of us has an assignment or purpose. Once again, your genetic composition is unique; your fingertips, blood type, chemistry—all make for a unique and very special human being; you are one unique person in a world of over six billion. The Bible says: "Thus saith the Lord that made thee, and formed thee from the womb..." (Isaiah 44:2 KJV)

#31: The Borrower Is a Slave To The Lender

This tip is from a Bible verse taken from the book of Proverbs. No matter how beneficial it might seem, debt – any kind of debt – leads to only one place: slavery. One definition of slavery is a state of being dominated. Whether it is a nation in debt or a simple loan between two kids at a playground, the net result is that the borrower shall always be bound in some form of servitude to the lender.

#32: Sometimes Life Will Challenge You To Take A Risk That Will Either Sink You Or Launch You

It is a fact that at some point, life will throw you a challenge: to maintain or roll the dice; to stay safe or walk on water. Renowned hockey superstar Wayne Gretsky observed, "You miss 100 percent of the shots you never take."

Our Journey: By B.J. Bohne

In other words, when you over-think your prospects, you become paralyzed and stop shooting altogether, thus increasing your chances of failure to 100 percent. On a recent trip to Russia, a friend said something that has stayed with me ever since. I was debating whether I should step out into another season of my life and he said, "Dennis, if you don't step out in faith to do what you are designed to do, you will miss the whole reason for your existence. And pretty soon, someone will take your place in history." This is an important tip. It actually explains why this company and many others like it have enjoyed such extraordinary success.

#33: Without Integrity, Business Arrangements Mean Little Or Nothing

The word integrity originates from a Latin word integer, which means inner strength. It can also be defined as moral soundness or the absence of duplicity. People of integrity are reliable, accountable and internally clean. The Italians have a proverb that says, "Between saying and doing, many a pair of shoes is worn out." All contracts are porous if the parties have no integrity. It remains the most vital factor in all decision making. Integrity is not built on some stage or in the limelight. It is not learned in a conference or seminar or taught in business school. Integrity is developed internally. Who you really are is determined by what you do and how you act, not necessarily by how well you talk or by what you say.

#34: To Grow With Balance, You Must Give Attention To Your Body, Soul and Spirit

When I talk about setting goals as a critical tool for success, most people immediately think about career advancement or financial gain. As magnets attract metal,

Imperial Crane

goals attract your dreams. They subsequently dictate what you give your time and efforts to. So, if you only have career goals, you will certainly make strides in that area, but your life will soon become imbalanced. In other words, you will focus on and devote the bulk of your time to your career and, like so many, you will neglect your family, your spiritual life and other important areas of development. So set spiritual, social, family, physical and career goals. It's the only way to enjoy a balanced ride to the top.

I Put My Hand On Destiny

I put my hand on Destiny
Said the tyrant to the Man.
I would rule the world my way ---
But to my dismay, I have found He had a plan.

I was cruel and selfish ---
Others mattered not to me.
I paid the price soon after
I put my hand on Destiny.
Said the tyrant, "How I suffered
When my sinful ways were found.
I needed Him to rescue me
From sins that had me bound."

I put my hand on Destiny
Said the bully to the Man
All the world would cower before me ---
But to my dismay there was another plan.

I put my hand on Destiny
Said the law-breaker to the Man.
The whole world was filled with chaos
Until He revealed his plan.

I put my hand on Destiny
Said the cheater to the Man
And Trust collapsed by failures
As seen throughout the land.

Our Journey: By B.J. Bohne

I put my hand on Destiny
Said the exploiter to the Man
But it didn't really end up right
Because, you see, He had a better plan.

Willadene
Angel Children, Rainbows of Love,
Dreams are Forever,
and other Poems
Copyright 1981

"Based on the gift they have received, everyone should use it to serve others, as good managers of the varied grace of God."

1 Peter 4:10

Chapter 9

Our Culture

"If we could not do a job safely, we were not going to do it at all."

– Fred Hunssinger

Crane operators face an extremely high risk of injury or death every day; their job has been classified as one of the most dangerous in America. John Bohne was a crane operator as were his father, brother, uncles and many of his closest friends. The intimate familiarity with the potential hazards he and others in the industry faced is what fueled John's desire for all crane operators to be able to get home to their families every night.

Before safety was the buzzword it is today, John had the words "Talk Safety" written on the sides of his cranes. Perhaps it was an outlook he brought to the field from his insurance background. Whatever the impetus for his philosophy, John recognized safety as an integral part of what he wanted to

Our Journey: By B.J. Bohne

do and knew that, ultimately, it would save him a lot of money and help him build an exceptional company.

Jesus, Please Help Me

It was a lovely sunny morning in Chicago. The kids were jumping on the trampoline and life felt grand. A text message came in on B.J.'s iPhone with a picture attached. It was a picture of one of his cranes – the unmistakable three hundred and sixty ton, $3 million, Leibherr all-terrain crane. Its backside had literally dug into a collapsed part of the street leaving part of its four hundred feet of boom hanging in the air.

Immediately, he called his friend and crane operator, Bob Kaleta.

"We've got a big problem," Bob said, "The street collapsed and the crane flipped over backwards. It's only hanging on by its counter-weight."

The crane was sitting in a narrow thirty-foot-wide alley between two high-rise buildings in downtown Chicago, one block west of famous Michigan Avenue.

Its boom had cut like a butter knife into seven floors of a thirty story skyscraper. A little more tilt, and there would be a calamitous disaster.

Imperial Crane

"It was 11:00 a.m. on a Saturday morning when I got the call that our crane had collapsed into the street. No one has x-ray vision; you can't always tell what is going on underground. Even the City of Chicago doesn't really know where everything is down there. Make no mistake: ours is a dangerous job. Thankfully, out of the entire workforce of the 15,000 member Local 150 Union, I know for a fact that we had the best operator in the seat that morning. First, he had made sure his outriggers were on stable, solid ground. Most importantly, he had also retracted most of the boom before he swung it around to telescope it back out. Had he not done that, it would have been an absolute disaster." – Bill Tierney

Fortunately, the top floors of the building were vacant so no one was hurt; yet.

By the time B.J. got to the scene, the guys had tried a series of maneuvers to rectify the situation; the least risky first. For the next twenty-four hours, they did everything they could, elevating the risk of a full-scale collapse with each failed attempt. Nothing worked. Quite simply, they couldn't shift, dislodge or in any way move the Leibherr.

The potential liability was staggering. Furthermore, this crane was the company's big moneymaker. If it went out of

Our Journey: By B.J. Bohne

commission, the company would be toast. Imperial Crane couldn't afford this; not now.

Because of the proximity to Chicago's bustling downtown and some of its premier attractions such as Millennium Park and The Bean, news of the incident quickly spread, attracting various media outlets. In no time, camera crews flooded the scene, monitoring every move. With the site mere yards from one of Chicago's commuter rail stations, the city temporarily shut the system down. The news wires read: CRANE DISASTER SHUTS DOWN METRO.

> "My bankers were calling me; panic was in the air. The City of Chicago was unnerved and decided to announce an emergency meeting for the following morning. This gave me some respite and an opportunity to get it fixed by then. As the hours rolled on, it was clear we were at our wits' end. I was thinking that I was beginning to prove I had what it takes to run this company."

> "A catastrophic crane accident in the middle of downtown Chicago, however, would be a definite showstopper. The best of our engineering techniques had failed. In my utter desperation, I lifted up my hands and cried, 'Dad, I need help with this one. Jesus, please help me. I can't do this.' At that moment a

Imperial Crane

thought occurred to me: 'Bring in the five hundred ton crane.'" – B.J.

They already had a two hundred, a one hundred twenty, and a fifteen ton crane on the scene. In a maneuver that would confound the best of civil engineers, all four cranes began to carefully shift and dislodge the Leibherr. Some pushed down while others pulled up with counterweights. At B.J.'s command, all of the cranes lifted the Leibherr, and in a thunderous crash the dislodged boom on the seventh floor swung out, coming within a foot of crashing into the adjacent building. With it came raining debris; one small brick had enough velocity to crack a skull. A cloud of dust rose in a scene that looked somewhat like the collapse of the Twin Towers on 9-11. Camera crews, the fire department and everyone else ran for their lives, except Imperial Crane's crew who seemed amazingly calm. Everyone remained at his station and on task.

Travel Tip:

God Can Make A Way Where There Seems None

"We now know that half of that narrow street was vaulted, so we actually had less room to work with than we originally thought. I give kudos to my guys. If only one of them had decided to run for their lives, like

Our Journey: By B.J. Bohne

everyone else did, the whole maneuver would have gone south. Though they certainly appreciated my leadership, they were the real heroes." – B.J.

When the dust settled, the Leibherr was hovering five feet in the air, thanks to the assistance of the other four cranes. After repositioning it and retracting the boom, they gently laid it back on the ground.

"Mission accomplished." announced B.J.

"Aside from a few scratches, the Leibherr looked great. Disaster had been avoided. Now, that was God. He had once again done what only He can do – a miracle." – B.J.

After everyone returned, obviously relieved, the City of Chicago wanted to know their next move. "My twenty guys and I have been at this for twenty-four hours now.

We are exhausted," B.J. declared, "Right now, we're going to the Park Grill across the street for some well-deserved cocktails and lunch." No one argued with them.

That successful rescue effort afforded B.J. instant credibility with his entire team. If they ever doubted his leadership, that event settled it.

Imperial Crane

John had built this company on the tenets of service, safety and commitment. Imperial Crane clearly delivered the same that day, and continues to do so.

A Bold Philosophy

Since its inception, Imperial Crane has been a cut above the rest with regard to safety. For forty years, the company has consistently gone above and beyond required industry safety standards.

For a while, the safety department had operated out of a small storage facility off-sight in Joliet, Illinois. Eventually, they decided to return back to the main office, working around conference tables and makeshift hubs.

Their main focus was proactive engagement with the company's everyday safety affairs, which included recording accidents, and monitoring man-hours worked, injuries sustained, and third party accidents.

As the company's client profile elevated to serve entities such as refineries, safety increasingly became a priority. Although the company had exercised stringency in safety, it was time to tighten up and raise the ante if Imperial Crane was going to compete at the next level.

Our Journey: By B.J. Bohne

The standard Federal Occupational Safety and Health Administration (OSHA) guidelines include all ground rules for oversight and construction safety regulations. It is worth noting that the first OSHA manual was only recently revised from its original 1971 version, having ignored - or, at best, not addressed - four decades of technical advancements and the impact those advancements should have had on safety rules.

Travel Tip:

Commitment to Excellence Demands the Resolve To Go Beyond Ordinary

Unfortunately, it took injuries and catastrophes to force the re-evaluation of those regulations. That is the crane industry – rigid and slow to change.

Even though Imperial Crane had always operated above OSHA stand-ards, it was clear they needed some-thing bolder and as a result, they developed their own specialized safety manual for the crane business.

To do this, Herb Harmon, head of the safety department at the time, and his team, took the more stringent require-ments of their high-risk clients, such as refineries, laboratories, and chemical plants, and used those benchmarks as a basis to form a proprietary philosophy above and beyond any previous safety threshold.

Imperial Crane

"We wrote our own safety manual and began an aggressive re-education drive, including regular safety meetings, workshops, and a print campaign. The idea was to get the message across that for Imperial Crane, discussing safety was not mere rhetoric. We wanted to instill a new safety culture, and as such, we would have no tolerance for unwarranted risk. We weren't expecting perfection - we knew even our best operators would have incidents - but by keeping safety in the forefront of everyone's mind, we knew we would drastically reduce the risk of catastrophe." – Fred Hunssinger

B.J.'s commitment to the new, more aggressive safety philosophy was firm. Imperial Crane would pass on any job if they could not do it safely.

In a tough economy, as it was at the time, that was a bold and potentially costly position to take; but he knew merely talking about it wasn't going to cut it.

"I started seeing small, even negligible incidents, such as fender-benders, occurring. I knew as small as those occurrences were, they would eventually lead to larger incidents. Initially, I let the individual departments deal with them, but as they compounded, I knew it was time for stronger measures."– B.J.

Our Journey: By B.J. Bohne

Immediately, he instituted a policy that no matter how small it was, any incident caused by negligence would be deemed punishable. If suspended, operators could not return to work until they had met with B.J. himself.

> "I didn't do this to reprimand them like some school teacher or to arbitrarily impose my authority upon anyone, but I wanted to make sure they really got it; that they understood our philosophy. I wanted to give them the opportunity to clearly understand our expectations, and also to allow them to communicate their understanding of the same. It was also an opportunity to discuss any other driving issues we needed to be aware of, such as drug, alcohol or family problems; again, not as a disciplinarian, but in a sincere desire to help them if I could. I also did this so in the event they did not correct their actions, and we indeed had to let them go, they would have no confusion as to the reason for their termination. In fact, at that point we would not even need to have a conversation. No matter what, we had to be safe." – B.J.

B.J. changed the company slogan to Talk Safety. Live Safety. "For Imperial Crane," B.J. declared, "safety was not going to be merely rhetorical. We had to live it."

That carried a lot of weight, and motivated everyone to step up. Those who chose to not adhere to their commit-

Imperial Crane

ments got fired. Did they file any grievances with the union, as would normally be the case? None. They knew their being fired was not our issue; they simply could not meet our expectations.

Initially, problems arose as the new philosophy began to take root and the leadership continued to bolster the enforcement of a new disciplinary structure. The potential for cover-ups was elevated; guys had to think twice before they came clean about a fender bender, for example.

Those who worked safely also got rewarded and promoted.

> *"We had to show the guys that we were committed to accountability; that at the end of the day, it was not about being the first to get back to the yard after a job, it was about being able to get back to the yard with all ten fingers and in one piece: safe."*
>
> *– Fred Hunssinger*

Consequently, in 2008, Imperial Crane had an entire year without a single work-related injury. That was unprecedented in the crane industry.

That doesn't mean everything was smooth sailing. One operator forgot to hydraulically suck in one of the outriggers,

Our Journey: By B.J. Bohne

and as he drove back to base through downtown Chicago he was scratching cars along the sidewalk.

Of course, they didn't know until their phones started lighting up. Not only did the company have some legitimate damage claims, but opportunists also jumped on the band-wagon looking to make a quick buck.

● ● ●

Travel Tip:

Hardworking People Generally Experience More Luck

● ● ●

Given the inherent dangers of the industry, some would call it luck that there hasn't been calamity after ca-lamity. B.J. prefers, though, to say it has been God's Hand. Regardless of how their impressive safety record might be interpreted, without a doubt the company's commitment to safety has paid good dividends for their reputation, bottom-line and, most importantly, for the operators and their families.

A Culture Shift

At Imperial Crane, safety was not merely an ideology or some dogmatic philosophy; it was culture. Their maxim became: You are going to work safe or you won't work at all.

296

Imperial Crane

"After we moved back, I told B.J., 'I have a vision for a little double-wide trailer, a temporary structure to house the offices for our safety department.' I believed this environment would provide a private atmosphere where we could offer critical, one-on-one attention to our operators. In addition, our space would house a stand-alone training center where we would conduct training classes, play instructional videos, and so much more." – Fred Hunssinger

B.J. jumped on it right away and within three months the safety training center was up and running. The hub houses a thirty person safety staff, entrusted to educate employees with seminars and packaged training. By creating a proactive safety curriculum, the company has built an incident and injury-free work environment, resulting in a record low Experience Modification Rate (EMR) of .61. EMR is a calculation used to determine the cost of previous injuries and the chances of future risk; the lower the number the better. Crane companies are not even eligible to bid on a job at a chemical plant, nuclear facility or oil refinery if their EMR rating is greater than 1.0.

The change has been revolutionary for Imperial Crane. Hundreds of operators have been trained there, but even beyond that, the separate training facility has afforded the team the opportunity to extend an OSHA approved safety training course to outside companies. The two and one half

Our Journey: By B.J. Bohne

hour course benefits those employers by ensuring their employee's training and knowledge meets the American Society of Mechanical Engineers (ASME) and OSHA requirements.

"One thing to keep in mind is that Imperial Crane hires operators from the union. When they come to us, they expect to get to work right away. But for us, it's important they get oriented into our culture first before we send them out on a job. Of course, that doesn't always go over well. We don't have weeks or months to do it, but before they can work for us, those guys know they cannot compromise on safety."

"They have to understand there is only one way Imperial Crane does business: we do work safely or we don't do it at all. We tell them, 'If you refuse to adhere to these clear safety standards, then you cannot work with us.' It's simply not negotiable. Why? We want to spot the accidents before they happen, not after."

– Fred Hunssinger

A Safe Company

"What separates us from other crane companies is our culture of safety. We prize it above everything. I still tell my operators every morning as we send them out, 'Be safe out there.' With so many man-hours without a single incident, I think its working." – John Tierney

Imperial Crane

Imperial Crane has delivered forty-two years of exceptional results with a near-perfect and unequalled record in the crane industry. In fact, at the time of this writing, the company has completed a large refinery job that demanded over twenty-five thousand man-hours each week. They executed the contract with unsullied delivery and zero safety incidents.

In an effort to maintain and improve their safety culture, and in order to be cognizant of the best practices employed throughout theirs and other industries, Imperial Crane is currently affiliated with the following organizations:

- I.S. Networld
- Pacific Industrial Contractor Screening (PICS)
- Disa Contractors Consortium
- North American Substance Abuse Program
- Builders Construction Resource Center
- Construction Data Services
- Three Rivers Manufacturers' Association (TRMA)
- Specialized Carrier & Rigging Association (SC&RA)

"We do more to ensure safety than any other company I know of. We are looking at almost three million man-hours without a single lost-time injury to date. But even with the best engineering, one cannot guarantee perfect safety. You cannot see the vaulted street, the manufacturing default or the unseen structural de-

Our Journey: By B.J. Bohne

fect. There are risks you cannot see with the naked eye. So, we have been fortunate that no one has ever been killed, maimed or seriously injured. At any rate, we don't just talk about it; safety is what defines us. It's a service we cannot bill anyone for, which is why most companies don't want to talk about it. How does a crane company quantify safety? How does it translate into money? How do you justify a $100 thousand safety specialist's salary? A person, or company, looking only at the short term would be hard-pressed to respond to these questions." – B.J.

"Our cranes have state-of-the-art audio systems, computers, and TV monitors. Really, it's like a plane cockpit in there. Our hundreds of cranes are updated regularly, with daily in-house checkups and yearly third party inspections. Trust me; if you're a crane operator working today, you want to work for Imperial Crane."

"With me, you will get to do what every crane operator wants to do most: return home safely every night. But, maintaining these standards is not cheap, and consequently, we charge more than the average crane company."

"When potential clients come to us for price comparisons, the first thing I say is, 'Thank you for your interest, but I'll save us some time."

Imperial Crane

"Guess who always returns back to us? Refineries, laboratories and reputable companies who are looking for excellence and safety. One thing is for sure, there are companies out there who care about this excellence and safety; if there wasn't, we wouldn't be in business today." – B.J.

Regarding the $50 million insurance coverage mentioned earlier, as a direct result of their stellar safety record, Imperial Crane does not pay any more in premiums than your average crane company.

In other words, for the same amount of money they are able to purchase ten times more insurance coverage than almost anyone else in the industry.

Once again, at the time of this writing, the company boasts almost three million man-hours without a single lost time injury. Whether that is an industry record is yet to be determined.

But one thing is for sure, Imperial Crane has set an enviable standard.

"I believe we have the best core group of crane operators in the country," says Bill Tierney. "I can't tell them that (although they will probably read this), but they are the finest."

Our Journey: By B.J. Bohne

A Minor Injury?

As B.J. and I sat down for breakfast with his family and a few friends, they decided to tell me about their adventurous weekend.

A couple of weeks ago, an Imperial Crane operator was walking out of one of the refineries at the end of his workday. A security guard noticed that he was limping.

"Are you okay?"

"Oh, I'm fine. I fell out of my crane today," replied the operator. "But I am fine. I'm an old cowboy, it's probably nothing."

As a matter of policy, any accidents, however minor, must be reported and critiqued. Knowing this, the security guard immediately alerted his contracts manager who alerted Bill Tierney at Imperial Crane headquarters of the situation.

"We've got two problems here," the contracts manager said. "First, we had an incident; but more importantly, it was unreported." "No problem, we are all over it," replied Bill.

"Our on-site safety manager is there right now. We will take all necessary measures to resolve this."

Imperial Crane

The contracts manager was unsatisfied with that answer. He expected Bill or someone with executive authority to jump on the next flight and get down to the refinery in case terminations were needed.

> *"I was traveling home from an outing in Lake Tahoe with our insurance guys, Tim Moller of Hub International and Steve Dark from Northwestern Mutual. All the while, I was reading the email exchange between my office and the refinery, and clearly there was an escalation of emotions, so I jumped in: 'Glen, this is B.J. Bohne, the president of Imperial Crane. I apologize for any confusion. I recognize the severity of this situation. I will personally be there presently to work through this to your satisfaction.'" – B.J.*

After he hung up, Iva Boncheva, B.J.'s executive assistant, went to work to book them on the next flight out; but she couldn't. Between the deteriorating weather and the impractical connections, they were left with one choice – a private jet.

Why not send someone else to take care of it, you might ask. B.J. felt this was bigger than a mere misstep or mishap and as such, it demanded his personal attention.

> *"My biggest challenge is to ensure clear and concise communication, whether that communication is from*

Our Journey: By B.J. Bohne

the customer to us or from us back to the customer, or even amongst us. In this case, there was a communication breakdown, and that responsibility fell squarely on my shoulders. I had to go. Someone who works for me did not clearly communicate our philosophy." – B.J.

They flew straight to the site at Hutchinson Airport in Borger, Texas, and right to the refinery.

"As soon as we touched down that Sunday night, I called an emergency meeting with my team. I immediately saw the lapses in protocol and judgment. The problem was my team; I had to face that and fix it. I spent the following day jumping in and out of meetings with senior executives, as the refinery scrutinized our response to the event. Everyone knew it was a minor accident, but they wanted to know what remedies and safety nets we would put in place to ensure non-reoccurrence; which we did to their satisfaction. When it was all said and done, the on-site safety manager and in-house project managers were immediately terminated. 'C'mon B.J.' one may say, 'Aren't you making a fuss over a small incident? What's the big deal?' No! In our industry, an event that might appear to be a small incident is not small at all. The stubbing of a toe, a trip, a sprain, a fender-bender; nothing is minor. To me, everything must be handled

Imperial Crane

as though it were a major incident because in the crane business, there are no minor incidents when it comes to safety. At any moment, lives could be at stake. My job is to assure our clients that we recognize safety as a non-negotiable. This is important to me and if anyone on my team cannot see that, they will not work for me."

"I recall a conversation I had with our pilot before touching down in Borger that weekend. I had asked him what his safety record was. '100%,' was his answer. I thought: exactly! Just like the airline industry, you cannot be a 99% safe crane company. You just cannot afford to be. There is no room for a brain lapse. You are either 100% on it, or you'll have a catastrophe at best, or, at worst, massive fatalities!" – B.J.

Imperial Crane has won the Specialized Crane and Rigging Association's safety award for seven consecutive years. This morning, he and his top staff flew back from Washington, DC where they were recognized by Citgo Petroleum Corporation for over 258,000 man hours with zero recordable injuries at one of their refineries.

Imperial Crane can say that all of their operators have returned from work every single day. God has given these guys the wisdom to recognize what needs to be done to run this company with an unmatched safety record.

Our Journey: By B.J. Bohne

"When we talk about my legacy, this is what I am most proud of: I have been able to maintain and even exceed the safety standard my father set for this company forty-three years ago. He had a habit of investing millions of dollars back into our fleet every year; something we will continue to do as we face a future wrought with challenges. I am confident we will continually outperform the competition by working safer and smarter with better equipment. Not only are we engaged in one of the most dangerous industries, we also work in the most treacherous of environments. We have allocated adequate resources to our safety department so they can do whatever they need to do, from hiring to procurement, in order to ensure an unparalleled level of excellence." – B.J.

"Imperial Crane is a local, mid-west based operation. The way we do business will not change. We will always be a safe, ethical, personable and financially sound company. Our challenge now is to reproduce our success across the country. To the extent we are able to do that, the potential for Imperial Crane will be unlimited!"- Dave Dobson

As Imperial Crane continues to extend its operations beyond Illinois to Indiana, Oklahoma, St. Louis, Michigan, Texas, and throughout the USA, the company is in the process of identifying local directors to advocate the same proprietary

Imperial Crane

methodologies that have helped fashion a truly unique culture. Without a doubt, Imperial Crane is braced for the next phase of its evolution into a nationwide company with operations from New York to Los Angeles.

Chapter Travel Tips

#35: God Can Make A Way Where There Seems None

When you reach the point where absolutely no one and nothing can help your situation, what then? Where do you go and who are you going to call? It is said that human extremity is frequently the meeting place with God. It makes for an unmatched rendezvous point with divinity. The Psalmist wrote: "I look up to the mountains—does my help come from there? My help comes from the Lord, who made the heavens and the earth" (Psalm 121:1-2 NLT).

#36: Commitment To Excellence Demands The Resolve To Go Beyond Ordinary

To be honest, it is much easier to be just good enough, mediocre, substandard, commonplace and ordinary. We generally prefer to take the path of least resistance. I have always said that there are two types of people who don't get anywhere in life: those who don't come to the table, and those who only come to the table. By pursuing a culture of safety, Imperial Crane chose to go beyond merely coming to the table. They chose to operate profitably, but also to go beyond and set industry standards. Excellence is doing your absolute best within your capacity. Vince Lombardi said, "The quality of a person's life is in direct proportion to their commitment to excellence, regardless of their chosen field of endeavor."

Our Journey: By B.J. Bohne

#37: Hardworking People Generally Experience More Luck

I find it curious that most of the people the world calls lucky are not idle or lazy; they are hard workers. No wonder Benjamin Franklin said, "Diligence is the mother of good luck." I like how Stephen Leakon put it. He said, "I am a great believer in luck, and I find that the harder I work, the more I have of it." So you want to be called 'lucky'? Then you roll up your sleeves and work hard.

#38: Hard Work Leads To Prosperity

This travel tip is taken from the book of proverbs. It says, "Good planning and hard work lead to prosperity, but hasty shortcuts lead to poverty" (Proverbs 21:5). Have you noticed that there is really no such thing as an overnight success? When Tiger Woods first hit the golfing scene, some in the media called him an overnight success. Little did they know of the many hours Tiger and his father had spent on the green honing and perfecting his incredible skills? Latin super-star Ricky Martin said, "Most people don't know that it took me fifteen years to become an overnight sensation." All successful companies or individuals must commit time to their craft, and by so doing, they reap the fruit of success. By working hard, Imperial Crane now enjoys an enviable position as one of the most successful crane companies in the world.

Your Life Becomes Forever

Your life becomes forever
The minute you are born.
You're part of a large tapestry
From which each of us is torn.

Your life becomes forever
Making up the endless reams
Of the fabric of mankind –
Worn thin at times it seems.

Willadene
What are the Songs of Love? And other Poems
Copyright 1981

"Now to him who is able to do immeasurably more than all we ask or imagine, according to his power that is at work within."

Ephesians 3:20 (NIV)

Chapter 10

Our Legacy

"Like his dad, B.J. constantly thinks outside of the box and often sees opportunities long before anyone else does."

– Pat Walsh

Someone asked B.J. recently, "Are you sad that your dad died too young?"

"Sure, it would have been awesome to have him here, but my dad did in sixty years what most people do in two hundred," he responded. When B.J. thinks about his father's legacy, he is reminded of Julius Caesar's powerful statement: "Better to live one day like a lion than one hundred years like a lamb."

Several years ago, we held a special Father's Day service in B.J.'s home in Oakbrook. I had asked him to say a few words about his dad and what fatherhood means to him. He wrote a moving tribute to his father and as he read it, there

Our Journey: By B.J. Bohne

was not a dry eye in the room. Recently, in one of our writing meetings, he pulled out from his desk that very same, now somewhat frayed, letter and read it back to me. It was every bit as moving as when he first read it to all of us:

> *"When Dr. Dennis asked me to say a few words at service, I didn't know exactly what to say. It became clear that Father's Day to me, unlike for so many people, wasn't merely a day for dads–or a mandatory day to spend with Dad, which for me growing up meant going somewhere to play golf with him. It's not that I didn't appreciate my dad, I did. I took it for granted that he would always be there, because he was. He wasn't always around the house when we were growing up, but I always knew if I needed anything, he would be there. Six years ago, he was diagnosed with cancer and very soon after that, he passed away while getting treatment in Germany. He was no longer there for me and the security I always had that he could be there to fix problems or to comfort me was now gone. Since my dad's passing, when confronted with problems or crises in my life, I have turned to my heavenly father, God, for comfort and support. I realize now how God must look at me for taking for granted that if I needed anything, He would be there for me. And it wasn't until both of my daughters came into my life, Kailey, and Willadene just over three weeks ago, that I figured out how my father, and many of*

Imperial Crane

our fathers, were always there for us and how we so often took them for granted. I love my daughters more than I ever thought imaginable. They are perfect in my eyes and always will be. So remember that when you are feeling bad about taking your fathers for granted." – B.J.

This is a chapter B.J. would probably remove if he could. He has wrestled with me over almost every paragraph in this book that highlights his part in the tapestry of this story. His modesty is impressive. Throughout our time together, he constantly speaks proudly about his remarkable team, his brothers, and the hardworking men and women at Imperial Crane. Walk through Imperial Crane with him and you won't be able to have an uninterrupted conversation, because every few steps, he will stop to greet the operators and staff by name, "What's up?" "How is it going?"

"B.J., he is one-of-a-kind to say the least. Thank God! It's a roller coaster for me. Sometimes I think he is the greatest, other times I want to fight him. Isn't that the way it's supposed to be? But he knows I love him and always have his best interest in mind. I told him a long time ago that I reluctantly went to work full-time for his father, and that this is never what I planned to do with my life. But after John died in 2003, I let B.J. know that my loyalty lies with him and this company, and if I ever left Imperial, I would likely leave the crane business all

Our Journey: By B.J. Bohne

together. I think the last ten years or so have demonstrated that to be true." – Larry Eckardt

"I really appreciate our team. I have hundreds of guys who have never worked anywhere else. It's not only because we pay them well, but they realize we are the standard bearers. There is nowhere better they can possibly work. I don't say this with arrogance but as a statement of fact. We have worked hard to be a cut above the rest. It's like if you want to be a Navy Pilot, you want to be a Blue Angel. Likewise, if you have to be a crane operator, you want to work with Imperial Crane." – B.J.

Travel Tip:

Success is a Team Sport

"From the constant phone calls, radio, and meetings, this is a fast paced job. My day goes by so quickly I don't even feel it. With two hundred and fifty men here, twenty there and twenty-seven other guys over there, it's a thrill. I haven't gone out of the building for lunch in twenty-five years."

"There is never a dull moment. And it's not only me. People move or retire, but they don't quit at Imperial Crane. We have near zero employee turn-over. I can speak for the rest of the team that it has been an un-

Imperial Crane

believable experience working here. The things we have done will forever stay with us." – John Tierney

"When people go to work for Imperial, they stay there because they are treated well. Whoever you are, you are made to feel welcome and part of the family. They will do anything they can to help you. You just feel valuable and wanted; why go anywhere else? Frankly, I am not shocked at how well the company has done." – Ron Selby Sr.

"I am not a micro-manager. Because of my communication training, I think I have been successful in communicating exactly what I expect from those who work for me. This means they also know when they are not doing what I expect from them. I don't ever have to fire anyone. They can clearly see the handwriting on the wall based upon their performance or lack thereof. Sure there are times when Bill Tierney will recommend that we let someone go, but that is not my normal practice at all. Come to think of it, I don't ever remember my dad firing anyone either (apart from myself, of course). People have left and come back for various reasons, but for Dad to say to someone, 'You're fired' is not something I ever remember hearing. My style is to clearly articulate expectations and standards, and in my experience, sensible people will

Our Journey: By B.J. Bohne

Ted Alden was going through a bitter divorce when one
of his cousins suggested that he hang out with B.J. Maybe
B.J. would encourage him; they could play golf together
and the distraction would help him.

> *"I was at my wits' end in a disintegrating marriage. I
> would go over to his house and sit and talk to him. We
> would enjoy a cigar and he'd listen to me. I cannot
> thank him enough for those days. I remember talking
> to him on the anniversary of my dad's passing. It was
> B.J.'s daughter Kailey's birthday. He had invited me to
> go golfing. So I tried to explain that I didn't think it was
> a day to celebrate. 'Well,' he said, 'Ted, why don't we
> turn it around. Let's remember him and use it as a posi-
> tive.' That touched me. He was right, and we did. If I
> was in trouble and I had only one person to call, it
> would be B.J. He is very loyal and dependable. He will
> do anything for you." – Ted Alden*

> *"I have been privileged to both witness and experi-
> ence B.J.'s amazing generosity. Having had the privi-
> lege of being around both he and his dad, I can see
> the similarities, such as his imposing aura. But he's not
> exactly like his dad; you are not afraid of him. In fact,*

Imperial Crane

*he often goes out of his way to make you feel com-
fortable." – Robert Kaleta*

"Along with the so many honorable, straight-up people,"
says B.J., "I have met many liars, crooks and shameless
backstabbers. It's all part of life and the business world.
Ultimately, you will be disappointed because you are dealing with faulty humans. But you focus on moving on and
doing the best you can."

A Fearless Leader

B.J. doesn't exhibit the typical egomania that character-
izes most accomplished CEO's.

As you walk into the company warehouse at their
Bridgeview headquarters, you are welcomed by a large
portrait of a man and a young boy sitting in a crane.

> *"People ask me all the time, 'How do your brothers
> feel about you putting that big picture of you with
> your dad right at the entrance of your offices?' They
> are surprised when I tell them that it's Dad and Lance,
> not me. I would never put my picture up there." – B.J.*

With that said, this remarkable story would be vastly different without his leadership. In other words, as solid as any

Our Journey: By B.J. Bohne

company is, the need for a steady hand at the wheel cannot be overstated.

> *"I've been here in good times - watching the company grow from a few cranes to hundreds - and I've also been here through some very difficult times. B.J. has delivered through both scenarios. The naysayers, the ones who thought he would fail, would say his success is due to the foundation his father laid. Yes, he had a great foundation to build upon, but he has, through bold moves taken at great risk, brought our company to a whole new level."*

> *"In fact, in the last ten years, we have expanded faster and grown larger than we had during the entire twenty years before that. It hasn't been easy; the growth of a great company never is. One thing is clear: this company would not be where it is today had it not been for B.J.'s bold leadership." – Robert Kaleta*

I'll echo what Robert says, and will add that if it wasn't for B.J.'s courageous leadership, this company may not be here at all. Leadership expert Dr. John Maxwell rightly says, "Everything rises and falls on leadership."

> *"B.J. has done an amazing job. For anyone to step up to the plate as he has is remarkable. I admire him as a*

322

Imperial Crane

visionary. He seems to have the ability to figure out where he wants to go. Simply put, we would not be where we are today if he hadn't taken the risks he took. Sure, he is fairly young compared to other CEO's of companies in our caliber, but in spite of that, we have a seasoned management team who have set clear priorities of safety and service in the market place and as a result, have established an excellent track record of delivery in the industry."

– Dave Dobson

"To me, B.J. is like the educated version of his father. He knows how to play, but also knows how to pay attention. He is a good businessman. He gets along with Bill and the guys love him. He has definitely taken the company to the next level. I am confident about their future." – Sam Palumbo

Like any effective leader, B.J. has a great assistant. Bulgarian-born Iva Boncheva was initially hired as Kailey's nanny in 2007. She now serves as B.J.'s executive assistant, handles his personal finances, chaperones, hosts, does the company payroll and so much more. She also serves as the general manager of his group of companies.

"There are three things that make B.J. rather special. First, he is an extremely smart, hardworking guy. I never complain about his workload because it's what peo-

Our Journey: By B.J. Bohne

ple like him do. You don't get that way by just playing golf. So, it is okay for him to relax and do the things he likes to do, like working out (which he never misses, even when we are out of town.) Second, he is generous. He donates to charities, orphanages, medical concerns, churches and ministries. Third, B.J. will tell you the truth even when it hurts. Some of the things I do, I have trained for. For the rest, I have learned the hard way. Thank God I have a kind and patient boss."

– Iva Boncheva

• • •

Travel Tip:

You Reap What You Sow

• • •

"I may be good at a lot of things, but I have never really thought of myself as being great at anything. I would not want anyone to think for one moment that I am an incredible expert or business specialist; far from it. If I could, I would love to step aside and have Dad back at the reins. But I can't. I stepped into such gigantic shoes. I still feel uncomfortable in his office."

"I run Imperial Crane with the thought 'If my dad walked in here again, what would he say?' Well, I kind of know what he would say first: 'Good job, but get out of my chair.' But seriously, I would like to think that he would say, 'Son, you have done a great job.'"

Imperial Crane

"I still have nightmares of him reprimanding me about some bad decision I've made. But I don't spend energy stressing about the size of our debt or the company's future. The one tool in my arsenal that never fails is this: I find my unwavering tenacity and desire to keep going by completely trusting in God. I trust that as I do my part, He will do His part – that part only He can do." – B.J.

The Girls

I have had the privileged of interviewing all of B.J.'s close friends for this book. What's intriguing is that they all seem to echo this sentiment regarding him: "B.J. is always able to compartmentalize. We could all go out to play, drink, party, but somehow, he seems to always know when he's had enough and when it's time to close shop and go home. He knows when it's time to get back to his family."

"I think we are hunters. My dad was a hunter. I am a hunter, and I am very good at it. Look around the house: the animals, the deals, the girls; I love it. I have dated some of the most beautiful women. I've flown to the Playboy Mansion in L.A. to pick up gorgeous girls. It's been a wild ride. But I am now at this settling down season of my life. Having two daughters has impacted me a lot. I have much greater respect for women in particular, knowing how vulnerable they

Our Journey: By B.J. Bohne

are. I am fearful for my girls. Will they meet jerks like I was?"

"There is nothing I wouldn't do to protect and provide for them. I also think a lot about my mother. I have such respect for her. With all her friends constantly asking her how she could put up with my dad, I applaud her for her incredible strength to keep our family together. It is the most unselfish act I have ever witnessed." – B.J.

Being around the Bohne house is refreshing. This is definitely a kid-friendly bachelor pad with trampolines, swimming pool, slides, play sets, and a fantastic basement. Our kids love going to Mr. B.J.'s house, as they call it. As we worked on this book, you could hear the pitter-patter of the girls' feet in the rooms above his home office where we hung out. Regularly, giggles and screams of joy permeated our oft-quiet moments. It was common to be interrupted by quiet taps on the door from Willadene wondering how long her daddy was going to be, or Kailey asking why Daddy was golfing again. I remember her innocent questions about this book, "What are you doing with my dad Dr. Dennis?" She wanted me to tell her exactly what I was going to do with all the research, and who I had talked to. She even wanted to read portions of what I had completed.

Finally, I thought I should ask her about her father.

Imperial Crane

"Oh, Dr. Dennis, I really love my daddy. I like getting up early in the morning, and going to the gym with him. I like climbing up on the machines as he works out. I love going bike riding. I love going to the movies with him, even watching videos here at home with him. I just love spending time with him. I like how he snuggles with me, and gives me a lot of bad tickles. I hate being away from him, especially when he has to go off to Arizona." – Kailey Bohne

I was impressed by her eloquence, so I asked if there was anything she didn't like about her father. Unhesitatingly, she said, "Well, the only thing I don't like about my dad is when he tells me things I don't want to do and how I have to be the one to always say sorry all the time."

B.J. walked up in time to hear his daughter's only complaint. It was cool to see him lean down and remind her of the many times he had said sorry to her. Then he turned to me and said, "My kids remind me of my relationship with God.

Sure I have business problems, but I find it pathetic that I spend all this time worrying about things going wrong or right. It's a shame I don't trust God like my girls trust me. It's a shame we keep worrying about things we can't even change. But, like God, I want to provide the most stable and safe environment for my kids."

Our Journey: By B.J. Bohne

"I spend large amounts of time with the girls. They are very bright. Without a doubt, I am looking forward to actually working with them in the future." – Iva Boncheva

Irena is the third girl in B.J.'s life. They met at the famous Crowbar, a club in Chicago. It was fight night and Robbie Gould, a kicker in the NFL at the time, was celebrating his new multi-million dollar contract.

B.J. walked up to Irena and asked to buy her a drink.

"We had a couple of drinks and then I excused myself. The following morning, I could not stop thinking about him. Two weeks later, I was out with my girlfriends at a totally different club when I saw him again. My heart started racing. The minute he saw me, he came right up to me and called my name, which surprised me. I guess I had left an impression. What were the odds? I hadn't been out since, and meeting him again in such a large city was crazy to me."

"After ordering the same drink he ordered for me two weeks prior, he said, 'I'm not leaving until you give me your number.' I did, and he texted me at 7:00 a.m. the following morning. Even though we were both attached in existing relationships, this felt right. We saw each other on and off, as I became slowly introduced

Imperial Crane

to his world. I really gave him room. I hadn't had good experiences with wealthy guys; I thought they were basically party animals full of themselves and unable to commit to a serious relationship. I wasn't looking for fun. I was looking for real love and real commitment. B.J. was different. He gave me 100 percent attention. Sure he was busy, running this huge company, but somehow he managed to make me feel special. He made me feel like I was the only one in his life." – Irena

B.J. was also ready to get serious with someone. Irena knew she could not control him or manipulate him to stay with her. When he pulled back, she would back off and let him figure out what he really wanted to do, whoever he wanted to be with, or if their love could survive and grow.

"I liked this girl; she was different, and special. We talked a lot and became real good friends. We had a lot of really good times together, and soon enough we started talking about family, about having a child or two." – B.J.

As the relationship grew, B.J. started talking to her about quitting her job. He wanted to take care of her, but she wouldn't let him, and for the longest time she kept her job until Willadene was born. Even then, she insisted upon returning to work.

Our Journey: By B.J. Bohne

"I have the utmost respect for him and I don't take anything for granted. He has been incredibly generous with me, but as I keep telling him, it's not the material stuff that I care for. I'm just grateful to have him in my life. He is a perfect gentleman: always telling me how he loves me, pulling out chairs for me, opening doors. I have been with him through some difficult times with the company. I remember his struggle with the banks. He was not panicked, although he took time to prepare me for the worst. I know he was looking for answers. Sometimes he couldn't sleep much at night. I would find him reading the Bible, which is one of the things that really drew me to him: his trust in God. God had guided him and the team with specific answers. It is clear that God has given him this success." – Irena

> **Travel Tip:**
>
> **It Is Pointless Worrying About Things We Cannot Change**

"Unlike me, Dad had zero tolerance for women intruding into business. This doesn't mean he was right; it's what he believed he needed to do to build his business. I remember feeling like a slave to my job. I would ask him to let me go spend some time with a girlfriend after a twelve hour day and he would say, 'No. We

Imperial Crane

have dinner scheduled with clients.' I knew what that meant. I would not be home till after midnight." – B.J.

Today, B.J. lives a very different life. It's almost 11:00 a.m. as we conclude our interview, and he is not on the clock in the office, because he does not need to be. He is "The Guy". We are enjoying a fresh fruit smoothie in his $5 million mansion in one of the country's wealthiest suburbs. He lives an enviable life only accessed by a small sliver of the world. He keeps checking his watch because today, like every day, he is going golfing. In a few minutes, he will be driving out in his Ferrari or Bentley or Mercedes. Clearly, long-gone are the twelve to fourteen-hour days. He has paid his dues.

"B.J. has successfully led this company to a level we never expected we'd achieve in less than ten years. And with the rise of the next generation of employees and teams throughout our management structure, the future of this company is limitless. I am proud to be part of the next phase of this company's expansion from a regional operation to a nationwide - even worldwide - company." – Larry Eckardt.

"Two years ago, I contracted pneumonia. My lung collapsed and I had a lot of health problems. It is only by God's grace that I am well today. The whole experience gave me a different attitude about life. In the process, I could not work for over six months. Although I work on a 100% commission basis, Imperial Crane

Our Journey: By B.J. Bohne

never skipped a payment to me. For me, this is more than a good paying job. I have met superstars, the governor, the mayor, senators, enjoyed big-ticket events, and had a blast the whole way. I often say this at our staff meetings, 'Guys, you will never find a company that treats you like this; not just because the checks are good. I love this company.' If I was only ten years younger, I would work a lot longer. For me, it all started 17 years ago. John Bohne has impacted my life. Every so often, I drop flowers off at his grave and I get to tell him, 'John, the kids are doing good!' When you look in my travel case, there is a card that I carry from his wake dated October 18, 2003, the day of his funeral, just so I remember him and what he did for me. Just so I can say yet again, 'Thank you, John!'" - Daryl Lutes

"As arrogant as this might sound to some readers, I don't have any regrets. Indeed, I am flawed like everyone else. I've had my share of ups and downs, victories and pitfalls. I have been married, divorced, hurt people, and been hurt by others; but, good or bad, I would not change anything; nothing at all. I believe God has a master plan for my life that transcends anything I have done or ever could do. I think I must trust His design, His plan and His future for me." – B.J.

Chapter Travel Tips

#39: Success Is A Team Sport

I have been privileged to meet some very powerful people; men and women who have built monumental organizations around the world. I have enjoyed a perusal of memoirs of yesterday's greats. At the end of many a rich life, they all seem to say the same thing: "If I were to do this over again, I would invest in the right relationships. I would not waste irredeemable time trying to please the wrong people. I would pour my life into those who were interested in my future. I would love my spouse more, play harder with my kids and be available to my friends." That is real success, and no one does it alone. Friend, you and I are made for relationship. We are not designed to walk through life alone.

#40: You Reap What You Sow

The Bible puts it this way, "Do not be deceived: for whatsoever a man sows that shall he also reap." In other words, life will give you what you put into it. I come from a farming tribe in Africa. We know that if you want good fruit you must sow good seed. You cannot sow bad seed and then get shocked that you have bad fruit. Also, you cannot sow bad seed, and then demand good fruit. To enjoy generosity, kindness and loyalty, B.J. applied himself in those areas.

Our Journey: By B.J. Bohne

#41: It Is Pointless Worrying About Things We Cannot Change

Two things strike me about worry; first, it is unnatural. You and I are not designed to worry. That's why it makes us sick. Worry is learned. It is not part of our personality or make-up. Second, worry is a pointless time-waster. It accomplishes absolutely nothing. Unlike any other time in history, a wide cross-section of this county is living under extreme duress and constant worry. Whether it is politics, climate change, loneliness, work overload, family frustrations or simply personal anxiety, there seems to be many reasons for every one of us to join this bandwagon of worry and depression. Hundreds of thousands will go to a doctor for worry-induced stomach issues every year. In fact, up to 90 percent of all doctor visits are for stress - a fancy name for worry - related issues. Stress has been linked to the leading causes of death in the country. Jesus said, "Can all your worries add a single moment to your life?" (Matthew 6:27 NLT) Of course not!

The Master's Plan

He has moved the massive mountains
Changed the rivers as they flow,
And he will change the gushing fountains
Of false information so the truth we'll know.

Eternal verities withstanding
May tend to come and go
And facts many soon be fiction
When the TRUTH begins to show.

It takes profundity of understanding
to pioneer research of the mind
And find what makes some cruel and evil
And others Good and Kind.

There's a message here for all of us
so find the Master's Plan
For putting Love and Gentle Kindness
Within the Soul of every man.

Willadene
The Master's Treasures
Copyright 2000

"Therefore I tell you, do not worry about your life, what you will eat or drink; or about your body, what you will wear. Is not life more important than food, and the body more important than clothes? Look at the birds of the air; they do not sow or reap or store away in barns, and yet your heavenly Father feeds them. Are you not much more valuable than they? Who of you by worrying can add a single hour to his life?

Therefore do not worry about tomorrow, for tomorrow will worry about itself. Each day has enough trouble of its own."

Matthew 6:25-27, 34 (NIV)

Epilogue

"Okay, here is an assignment for you. I want you guys to list on a fresh piece of paper, the main things you want to accomplish over the next ten years. Get it to me and I will mail it back to you later," announced my high school English teacher, Mr. Ozinga.

Here is what I wrote:

> - ❖ **I will go to Arizona State University**
> - ❖ **I will graduate with my degree**
> - ❖ **I will work at Imperial Crane**
> - ❖ **I will run Imperial Crane**

Years later, I found that piece of paper that Mr. Ozinga had mailed back, and, to my astonishment, every single one of those goals had been achieved. In fact, I wish I'd written more.

When I took Imperial Crane over, my primary objective was to not screw it up. I didn't want to be the guy who wrecked the ship or killed the golden goose. While some might want to chop it up, strip it and sell it off for its value, my job was (and still is) to keep it alive and healthy; to keep it "laying eggs" so every one of us is sustained. I can say that I

Our Journey: By B.J. Bohne

have far exceeded my own expectations, and for that, I am so thankful to God.

In this book, we have tried to articulate some of the most important elements of our journey, both as a family and a business. There is so much we have left out, and maybe some things that some readers, even I, wished we hadn't included. But here we are.

It has not been my intention to give the impression that I am anywhere as good as my dad. I am not John Bohne. I could never be John Bohne. No one can. To me, he was in a league of his own. It's been nine years since he passed away. I still miss him. Our family misses him. His friends miss him. We all, even my daughters who never got to meet him, wish he were still with us.

We recently went to the cemetery where he is buried to pay our respects. It was moving when Kailey led us in a prayer for her Grandpa John. It gives me some comfort knowing that this book will help her, and her own kids years from now, to know him a little better.

John Bohne lived life to the fullest. He worked hard and also played hard. When he popped the cork on that $200 bottle of Chateau Le Fit, you can bet he enjoyed every sip of it. This is one thing we can all take away from his life: he enjoyed it. Again, Dad lived everyday to the fullest.

Imperial Crane

I was moderating a staff meeting recently when suddenly my thoughts meandered away from the room. I was filled with appreciation for our business and its success; the nice office facilities we had; the four decades of momentous accomplishments. "Look what we have been able to achieve," I thought. As I was basking in that glow of gratitude, someone voiced a complaint about some ongoing project. I'm not one to evade issues, but at that moment I didn't want to focus on the negative. I thought we needed to be more appreciative of the blessings God has given us.

Yesterday, another very loyal employee sent me an email. She wanted to know if she would have a job after a large contract that she is supervising comes to end. Even though she has worked with our company for years prior to this project, she was still concerned. Of course I assured her that her job was safe, but I wondered why she would think otherwise.

At any given day, Imperial Crane has hundreds of cranes working on jobsites all over the country in the most treacherous environments. Any one of those cranes could have a major accident right now. Do I have cause to worry? You bet I do. But what would that accomplish for me? Nothing. Worry is really one of the most pointless emotions. In fact, it's a total lack of faith for me to keep giving into it, and I kick myself every time I do.

Our Journey: By B.J. Bohne

I sometimes imagine an eighty-five-year-old, silver-haired B.J. reminiscing about this journey on some porch at a ranch in the country somewhere. I know for a fact that I will regret all the times I have wasted by stressing over "stuff." C'mon, how bad do we really have it? Look where we live; what we have. So what if the sun isn't out today or we have to contend with some snow or sleet. So what if we have some bills to pay? How bad do we really have it?

If you only take one thing from this book, please consider this: stop and enjoy today. This very moment. Now. Stop dwelling on what's going wrong, and praise God for what's going right.

If we dwell on what we don't have, we are sure to miss what we do have: our families, health, friends, opportunities, our nation, and the innumerable precious moments that will never return.

I relate to the great King Solomon quite a bit. He is said to be the richest man who ever lived. He had palatial homes, beautiful vineyards, magnificent parks, lush gardens, hundreds of servants, great herds and flocks, heaps of gold and silver, one thousand wives and concubines, and great fame. In fact, he said that he had, "everything a man could desire."

Imagine that for a moment.

Imperial Crane

But at the end of his superfluous life, King Solomon wrote:

"... But as I looked at everything I had worked so hard to accomplish, **it was all meaningless**. It was like chasing the wind. There was nothing really worthwhile anywhere." (Ecclesiastes 2:8, 11 NLT)

Then he said, "... here is the conclusion of the matter: Fear God and keep his commandments, for this is the duty of all mankind." (Ecclesiastes 12:13 NIV) This great king had reached the same conclusion as I and many others have: true happiness isn't attained by the proverbial chase for status, fame or net-worth.

I recently watched a broadcast service by Joel Osteen. He talked about God opening and closing doors for us. Often, we get crushed when things we perceive as opportunities vanish; we have had a few of those through the years.

God will sometimes close doors, and even though we may think it's a bad thing, He knows better and is always looking out for us. We must be faithful and simply put our trust in Him.

What a journey this has been. And like any journey, the end is yet to be written. Who knows if the door may one day

Our Journey: By B.J. Bohne

be closed on Imperial Crane? But for now, God has chosen to bless this company, and only He knows what the future holds. Meanwhile, I will be faithful to both the doors He opens and the ones He closes.

As I bring this book to a close, I would be remiss if I didn't mention our continuing efforts to honor Dad's legacy by championing his generous spirit even to those who have never heard about him. To this day, I am still stumbling upon his private acts of benevolence. He did not believe in parading his generosity. From feeding a helpless family, paying off a crane operator's debt, hiring attorneys to defend the defenseless, to re-roofing a small local church, Dad had a big heart.

Beyond the sterling safety record and phenomenal growth of Imperial Crane is a desire to contribute to the betterment of the needy members of our global citizenry. Every year, Imperial Crane sends ten under-privileged kids to a summer camp. For over five years, we have donated Christmas presents to over one hundred orphans at the *SOS Family Village* in Lockport, Illinois. My desire has been to give these kids gifts that others in their situation would never get, such as iPods, high-end videogame consoles, laptops, and so on. I also serve as co-chairman of *Muscle Team Chicago*, a Muscular Dystrophy Awareness program, for which we have raised over $700,000 in the last two years.

Imperial Crane

To this end, I have created a charity, The *Bohne Foundation*, through which I and many of my friends get to give back in service to the neediest members of society. We are actively involved in charity work from as far away as Uganda, in the middle of Africa, to local communities right here in Chicago, Illinois. Whether it's drilling a water well, building a school or hospital, sending troubled kids to youth camps, or funding medical research, we are determined to make a difference in the lives of those who can't - those who don't have. Please visit our website (www.bohnefoundation.org) for further details.

Once again, I salute all the dedicated men and women of *Imperial Crane Services* for journeying with us. I will leave you with these words from the greatest book ever written:

> *"For in him all things were created: things in heaven and earth, visible and invisible, whether thrones or powers or rulers or authorities; all things have been created through him and for him. He is before all things, and in him, all things hold together."* (Colossians 1:16-17 NIV)

Words of Truth Have Been Written

Many words of truth have been written
Through ages and ages before
But people forget the obvious
And need be reminded once more.

The good lives forever –
The bad dies with time.
Why waste the hours given
When each day is sublime.

Find the right pattern early in life –
Create an island of peace in each day.
all the pitfalls leading to strife –
Search for right values and be on your way.

Willadene
What are the Songs of Love? And other Poems
Copyright 1981

"If I could speak all the languages of earth and of angels, but didn't love others, I would only be a noisy gong or a clanging cymbal. If I had the gift of prophecy, and if I understood all of God's secret plans and possessed all knowledge, and if I had such faith that I could move mountains, but didn't love others, I would be nothing. If I gave everything I have to the poor and even sacrificed my body, I could boast about it; but if I didn't love others, I would have gained nothing. Love is patient and kind. Love is not jealous or boastful or proud or rude. It does not demand its own way. It is not irritable, and it keeps no record of being wronged. It does not rejoice about injustice but rejoices whenever the truth wins out. Love never gives up, never loses faith, is always hopeful, and endures through every circumstance…

<u>And the greatest of these is love.</u>"

1 Corinthians 13:1-7, 13 (NLT)

About B.J.

Entrepreneur/Business Executive/Philanthropist
Born: 1970; Birthplace: Palos Height, Illinois, USA

B.J. Bohne grew up around the family crane business. He worked in shops and operated cranes as he helped build **Imperial Crane**, a company his father John Bohne founded with a single crane in 1969.

In 1992, he joined Imperial Crane's management team after graduating with a Bachelors degree in communication from Arizona State University.

Since his father's passing in 2003, B.J. has led **Imperial Crane Services** as president and CEO. The award-winning company has grown under B.J.'s leadership from eighty employees to over five hundred, increased its fleet from thirty to over three hundred cranes, and has nearly quadrupled its revenues from $30 million to well over $100 million, elevating its prominence from Chicago's largest crane company to one of the largest crane companies in the world.

B.J. Bohne is also the founder & CEO of the Dallas-based **Crane Network**, the number one online resource for used cranes since 1998.

These accomplishments, in addition to his successful investments in several other businesses across the country, make him, irrefutably, one of America's top young business titans.

He serves as an avid philanthropist through his charity, **The Bohne Foundation**, dedicated to needy children, educa-

Our Journey: By B.J. Bohne

tion, medical research, and to serving the needs of local communities around the world.

B.J., daughters Kailey and Willadene, and his fiancé Irena, live in Oakbrook, Illinois.

Note From the Author

When I got home that January afternoon after my lunch appointment with B.J. Bohne, I was somewhat befuddled. I had just committed months of my life to writing a story about a family business I knew very little about, save the massive billboards along Chicago's freeways. I thought, "Dennis! With your hectic schedule, where will you find the time to do the necessary research for this book?" Meanwhile, my discerning wife picked up on my disquietedness. Ingrid said, "Honey, you've gotta do this! It will help many people, and it will be very good for you." And boy was she right!

These last few months have been incredible. Pouring hundreds of hours into this family's rich history and immersing myself into the powerful story of a dreamer, John Bohne has been incalculably inspiring. And what an honor it is for me to witness the continuation of his story through a son who has stepped up and rallied his brothers and team to carry John's baton after his tragic decease. Together, and to everyone's astonishment, they have quadrupled John's success.

Why did we write this book? Certainly not for fame, profit or vanity. Indeed, life itself is a journey. Wherever you are today is not necessarily where you will be tomorrow. The travel tips that we have extracted from *Imperial Crane's* journey are universal. Use them and share them with others. It is our desire that in some way, this book will offer healing to a broken spirit, inspiration to a weary heart, and warmth to a

Imperial Crane

tired soul. May you find courage as you face the difficult and sometimes chaotic seasons of your own life.

Dr. Dennis Sempebwa

www.e-wings.net
Twitter: @dsempebwa
YouTube.com/drdshow

About the Author

For over three decades, Ugandan-born Dennis D. Sempebwa has served in sixty-three countries.

Dubbed one of Africa's new breed of pragmatic leaders, Dennis is a consultant, management trainer, sought-after speaker, counselor, and an advisor to several organizations around the world. He holds two master's degrees and three doctorate degrees, including two Ph.D's. His books and media broadcasts reach millions around the world.

Dennis, his beloved wife Ingrid and their five children reside in Chicago, USA.

Contact:

Imperial Crane Services

1-888-HOIST IT

www.imperialcrane.com

Illinois Address:

7500 W. Imperial Drive,

Bridgeview, IL 60455

Tel: (708) 598 2300

Fax: (708) 598 2313

Indiana Address:

1349 E. Main Street,

Griffith, IN 46319

Tel: (219) 924 2900

Fax: (219) 924 3800

Missouri Address:

300 Washington Street

S. Roxana, IL 62084

Tel: 1-888-HOIST IT

Texas Address:

3929 FM 1090

Port Lavaca, TX 77979

Tel: 1-888-HOIST IT

Contact us:

Eagle's Wings Press
A Division of Hunter Heart Publishing™
1510 Chiles Ave. Suite 7
Fort Carson, Colorado 80913

publisher@hunterheartpublishing.com

(253) 906-2160

www.hunterheartpublishing.com